USE THE MOST EFFECTIVE SYSTEM FOR
RUNNING MEETINGS EVER DEVISED . . .
NEWLY UPDATED FOR THE 21st CENTURY

Discover:

- How to run a meeting, from calling to order to adjournment
- Quick-find rules, troubleshooting guides, and helpful memory aids for using parliamentary procedure
- Expert tips to help the smart member or officer defeat or pass a motion
- Steps to create committees, get superior committee productivity and avoid committee misuse and abuse
- Directions for writing an outstanding committee report
- A checklist for taking and distributing complete, professional minutes
- Easy-to-follow rules to ensure a fair debate . . . and no long-winded speeches
- Do's and Don'ts for the successful chairperson
- Secrets for controlling an unruly or hostile meeting
- Procedures for officers and members to deal with an arbitrary or dictatorial chairperson

. . . and much more

THE DEMANDS OF THE 21st CENTURY WORKPLACE
REQUIRE FAST RESULTS AND SMOOTH COMMUNICATIONS. FIND OUT HOW TO MAKE MEETINGS A PLACE
YOU CAN PRODUCTIVELY CONDUCT BUSINESS,
SHARE IDEAS AND INFORMATION, AND MAKE DECISIONS WITHOUT WASTING TIME, WITH...

21st CENTURY
ROBERT'S RULES OF ORDER

Dear Laurie,

Congratulations for being chosen to represent the American Legion Auxiliary at Empire Girls State and for being honored as Poppy Queen for the year 2002 –

Barbara Pierce
Chairman American Legion Auxiliary Unit 304 Manhasset.

—21ST—
CENTURY
ROBERT'S RULES
OF ORDER

EDITED BY THE PRINCETON LANGUAGE INSTITUTE

LAURIE E. ROZAKIS, PH. D., COMPILER
ELLEN LICHTENSTEIN, SPECIAL CONSULTANT

Produced by The Philip Lief Group, Inc.

A LAUREL BOOK

Published by
Dell Publishing
a division of
Bantam Doubleday Dell Publishing Group, Inc.
1540 Broadway
New York, New York 10036

Published by arrangement with The Philip Lief Group, Inc
6 West 20th Street New York,
New York 10011

ISBN: 0-440-21722-9

Printed in the United States of America

Published simultaneously in Canada

November 1995

10 9 8

OPM

Contents

1

Introduction to Parliamentary Law

THE FUTURE WORKPLACE

Everywhere we turn today, growing complexity is increasing the pressure on our time. Businesses face new complexity, increased competition, and work force diversity. These pressures will only increase in the years ahead.

SUCCEEDING IN THE 21ST CENTURY

The people who succeed in the future will be those who best manage their time. The key to using your time wisely is simple—improve your efficiency and effectiveness. Technology has helped boost our efficiency, but it has not sharply affected our effectiveness. The mechanics of time planning have improved tremendously, thanks to the outpouring of planning books, forms, and computerized notebooks. These aids enable us to account for every minute of our lives. We can coordinate our schedule with those of colleagues so that we can schedule seemingly countless meetings. No doubt we have become more efficient at using our time—but not necessarily more effective.

While mechanical efficiency is unquestionably valuable, many aspects of business cannot be rushed.

Now, as in no other time in our history, businesses depend on effective decision making to keep pace with competition at home and abroad. The world of the 21st century demands new approaches and innovative thinking—especially when dealing with people.

In the 21st century, team playing will be essential; as a result, effective meeting planning and management will be crucial to business success. This is especially true with the technology explosion, as we stand on the brink of the most competitive and high-tech society the world has ever known. As companies streamline to keep pace with these changes, each individual's participation in meetings becomes more evident—and far more important.

The watchwords of current management philosophy are *total quality management* and *reengineering continuous improvement,* as many businesses are using small-group settings and workshops in an attempt to become more productive. It's clear that these goals can be achieved only through group dedication to common aims and priorities. Group members need a way to deal with each other that allows them to be both efficient and effective. Since the old ways are no longer working, managers and supervisors have begun looking for new methods to help people cooperate and work together smoothly. What's needed is a *recognized* method for running meetings smoothly. In business, public life, and community service, it's becoming increasingly clear that the key to a successful meeting is parliamentary law.

PARLIAMENTARY LAW IN THE 21ST CENTURY

More and more businesspeople are beginning to see the need for a system of codified rules to help order their meetings. Parliamentary law fulfills this vital need. If you had a dollar for every business meeting you attended that dragged on and wasted everyone's time, you would now be happily retired. The usefulness of parliamentary law in government and community affairs is unquestioned. What is becoming plain is that parliamentary law also provides a way for people in industry to conduct business quickly and fairly. It can help transform interminable, unproductive meetings into useful and efficient gatherings. These qualities position parliamentary law on the cutting edge of tomorrow.

Any deliberative assembly can tailor the rules of parliamentary law to suit the needs of a particular business. The organization need only adopt its own written rules in the form of a *constitution* and *bylaws*. Increasingly, more and more businesses are doing just that. This book will help you learn parliamentary law and learn how to adapt it to the needs of your own organization.

How parliamentary law can be used. Parliamentary law can be used to help people run an astonishingly wide variety of meetings. Here is a sampling:

- Teleconferences
- Service groups
- Shareholder meetings
- Library boards
- Department meetings
- Budget meetings
- Seminars
- Sales meetings
- Videoconferences
- Civic associations
- Scientific groups
- Board meetings
- Regional or national conferences
- Parent–teacher organizations

- School boards
- Garden clubs
- Senior citizen groups
- Advertising presentations
- Youth groups
- Small board meetings
- Historical societies
- Charitable organizations

What this book can do for you *and your organization in the 21st century.* This book is designed to help you run more effective daily and annual meetings, consultations, task forces, seminars, and sales conferences—all the demands of the 21st century workplace. It can also be used in any organizational meeting where a standard parliamentary procedures handbook is required.

This book avoids the stilted academic prose that makes some other guides to parliamentary procedure sound like dry-as-toast legal briefs. Rather, the *21st Century Robert's Rules of Order* uses everyday business language to explain how to ensure that meetings are productive for everyone.

ORIGINS OF PARLIAMENTARY LAW

Originally, *parliamentary law* referred to the customs and rules of conducting business in the English Parliament. The rules provided for the following guidelines:

- Treat one subject at a time.
- Alternate between opposite points of view in discussion.
- Always have the chair tally votes for both sides of the issue.
- Maintain decorum in discussion.
- Confine debate to the merits of the question under discussion.

These rules applied to what is called a *deliberative assembly,* a group of people meeting to decide on a common action. Never shy about borrowing a metaphorical cup of sugar from a former "relative," America adopted these rules to order its own system of representative government, the House of Burgesses.

Thomas Jefferson's Manual, Cushing's Manual. In 1801, during his term as president, Thomas Jefferson published the first book on parliamentary law, *Manual of Parliamentary Practice.* Explaining his actions, Jefferson wrote, "The proceedings of Parliament in ancient times, and for a long while, were crude, multiform, and embarrassing."

This was the primary source for parliamentary law until 1844, when Luther Cushing, clerk of the Massachusetts House of Representatives, published his *Manual of Parliamentary Practice: Rules of Proceeding and Debate in Deliberative Assemblies.* The book soon came to be called "Cushing's Manual."

Soon, parliamentary law was being used at all levels of government, from federal—Congress and the House of Representatives—to state, municipal, town, and village assemblies. But the rules still had not been modified to apply to the specific needs of running a club, service organization, or school meeting.

Robert's Rules of Order. Henry Martyn Robert, an army engineer, took on this task, and in 1876 he succeeded. He originally envisioned a folio of about 16 pages; the final volume had nearly 200 pages. Adding his name to the title, the general published *Robert's Rules of Order.* The entire print run sold out in four months; by 1915, more than 500,000 copies were in circulation. The book became *the* parliamentary law guidebook for organizations, schools, and clubs. People eagerly embraced a system that would help them run efficient, fair meetings. Now there was a way to control dictatorial chairpeople and overbearing members, time-wasting filibusters and destructive behavior. Parliamentary law helped guarantee that the will of the majority would prevail while the rights of the minority were protected.

Now we have updated these rules to apply to the 21st century workplace. While retaining the cornerstones of parliamentary laws, we have added what you need to know to run efficient meetings. In addition to information on the tried-and-true traditions of *Robert's Rules of Order,* such as motions, officers, and minutes, you will find sections on setting up annual conventions, booking meeting rooms, balancing budgets, and setting up the latest technology. The past meets the present to create the future!

WHAT IS PARLIAMENTARY LAW?

Parliamentary law is a system of rules that are designed to protect the rights of those people attending and running a meeting. The basic provisions of parliamentary law are quite simple:

- Ensure the right of the majority.
- Protect the rights of the minority.
- Defend the rights of individual members.
- Safeguard those people absent from the meeting.
- Guard all these together.

A deliberative assembly is free to do whatever it must to ensure these protections to all members. It is the best method we have to safeguard the rights and responsibilities of everyone at a meeting. To guarantee these prerogatives, parliamentary law requires participants in a meeting to do the following:

- Treat one item at a time.
- Extend courtesy and fairness to all.
- Let the majority rule.
- Guarantee the rights of the minority.

COMMON PARLIAMENTARY LAW TERMS

A complete list of all the terms used in parliamentary law appears in Chapter 10. To make sure that we are all speaking the same language right from the start, the following are brief definitions of the most common terms you will encounter in this book. Read the terms and the definitions over carefully before you go any further. Many of the terms are common in everyday life, but they are used differently in parliamentary law.

Term	*Parliamentary Law Definition*
Accept a report	Adopt a report, not just receive it.
Adjourn	End a meeting officially.
Agenda	List of items of business that the people attending a meeting consider.
Amend	Change a resolution or a motion by adding, striking out, or substituting a word or phrase.
Assembly	Organized group of people meeting to conduct business.
Ballot	Written vote that assures the secrecy of the individual's election decision.
Bylaws	Set of rules by which an organization conducts business.
Chair	Presiding officer of an organization, usually the same as the president.
Congress	U.S. House of Representatives (not the Senate).
Debate	Discuss the merits of a specific question.
Floor	Right of a person to speak to people at a meeting and have their undivided attention.
Main motion	Method of introducing new business to an assembly.
Majority	More than half of the members voting on an issue.
Meeting	Assembly of members gathered for any length of time without taking a recess.

Minutes	Record of the events of a meeting.
Motion	Proposal for action by the group.
Objection	Occurs when a member is strongly opposed to the main motion.
Order of business	Order in which the items on the agenda are discussed at the meeting.
Point of information	Request for an immediate answer to a question concerning the background or content of a motion or a resolution.
Point of order	Objection raised against any proceeding or motion that the member decides is a violation of the rules.
Point of personal privilege	Request for the immediate consideration of a matter that affects the comfort, safety, or orderliness of a member.
Precedence of motion	Claim of a motion to the "right of way" over another motion.
Previous question	Motion requiring an end to debate and asking that a vote be taken on the question being discussed.
Quorum	Number of members needed to conduct business.
Recess	Short break in a meeting.
Refer to committee	Create a committee or instruct an existing committee to do research and report its findings back to the group.
Rescind	Make a motion to nullify a vote taken at a previous meeting.
Second	Indication that a member wants a motion discussed by the membership.
Session	All meetings, even those that were adjourned.
Shall the question be discussed?	Mode of stating the question about considering a subject.
Substitute	One of the five forms an amendment can take.
Table	Motion to place a main motion and all pending amendments aside temporarily with the intention of bringing them back at a later time for action.

Two-thirds vote	What occurs when twice as many people vote "yes" as vote "no."
Unanimous consent	What occurs when no one objects to a motion.
Unfinished business	Matter that may have been pending at the time that the previous meeting was adjourned.
Withdrawal of a motion	Decision by a person who has made a motion to take it back.

RIGHTS AND RESPONSIBILITIES OF MEMBERS

Rights. Parliamentary law protects the rights of members to be dealt with fairly and equitably. This encourages everyone's co-operation and the timely order of business. Following are the member rights guaranteed under parliamentary law:

- Receive notices of meetings.
- Attend meetings.
- Make motions.
- Second motions (when they need a second).
- Debate motions (when they can be debated).
- Vote on motions (except those on which the person has a conflict of interest).
- Nominate people for office.
- Be nominated for office.
- Elect people to office in the organization.
- Be elected to office in the organization.
- Know the meaning of the question people are debating.
- Object when rules are being violated.
- Appeal the decision of the chair.
- Not have to suffer personal abuse and attack.
- Have access to minutes of all meetings.
- Receive the treasurer's report.
- Get a copy of the organization's bylaws.

Responsibilities. Along with rights come responsibilities. For a meeting to function smoothly under parliamentary law, members must have specific obligations as well. When all members understand their duties as part of a team, business will be accomplished with much greater ease. Following are the responsibilities of members under parliamentary law.

- Attend meetings.
- Be on time.
- Stay until the end of the meeting.
- Be ready to talk knowledgeably and intelligently on a topic.
- Be attentive.
- Be open-minded.
- Treat everyone with courtesy.
- Speak openly, but also let others have their turn to speak.
- Follow the rules of debate.
- Make a point concisely.
- Attack issues, not people.
- Insist on law and order at meetings.
- Work to create dignity and decorum.
- Participate actively in the meetings.
- Work with others in a cooperative fashion.
- Be familiar with the basic rules of parliamentary law.
- Obey the rules of the organization.
- Pay all dues and assessments.
- Respect the rights of others.
- Abide by the final decision of the majority.
- Bring in or recommend new members.
- Be familiar with the organization's bylaws.
- Select well-qualified officers.
- Participate in committees.
- Vary committee work.
- Respect the chair's opinions and rulings.
- Promote the organization's growth and influence.
- Enhance the organization's reputation.

HOW TO USE THIS BOOK

The *21st Century Robert's Rules of Order* offers you the following important features:

- How to introduce business
- How to obtain the floor
- Key methods to organize meetings
- How to make a motion
- What motions must be in writing
- Ways to create a committee
- How to chair a committee
- How to be a useful member of a committee
- Methods of voting
- Ways to conduct meetings
- Duties of officers
- How to move business quickly and fairly
- How to debate an issue
- How to write a committee report
- How to set up an organization
- How to run the first meeting
- Ways to elect officers
- Customs observed by officers and members
- How to create bylaws
- Legal rights
- Information on new meeting technology

2

Introduction to Business

You are a busy person and you want to get your meeting started as soon as possible. How can you bring business before an assembly? Let's see how it is done.

HOW TO INTRODUCE BUSINESS

There are only two ways to introduce business to people at a meeting: by making a *motion* or through *communications*.

Making a motion. A *motion* is a formal proposal by a member that the people in a meeting take action on a specific matter. The term *take action* is misleading, for some motions request specific action while others only express a point of view. Motions that bring business before the people in a meeting are called *main motions*. Other motions, in contrast, ask that the members consider the way business is done. These motions center on points of parliamentary procedure. (The process of making a motion is described in Chapter 3, "Motions.")

Using a communication. After a member or committee chair delivers a report, another member may introduce business in writing. This can be in the form of a memo or a letter addressed to the chair or to the president of the organization. Increasingly, the communications will be sent through E-mail, fax, or other electronic means. Usually, the clerk reads the letter or memo aloud. If the communication is of a sensitive nature, the chair will usually read it privately first. Reading the communication aloud to those present at the meeting, however, is not sufficient to bring business before the group; a motion must be made to consider the matter. Most often, this method is used when the member desiring to introduce business is not present at the meeting.

HOW TO OBTAIN THE FLOOR

Before you can bring a matter before people in a meeting, you must *obtain the floor*—that is, be recognized by the chair as having the right to be the only person speaking at that time.

To obtain the floor, you must rise, address the chair, and wait for the chair to acknowledge your presence. In a small, informal meeting, the chair might just nod in your direction or say your name as a form of acknowledgment. In a larger, more formal meeting, the chair is more likely to say your name and repeat your professional affiliation.

Example

A small meeting
A member says: "Madame President," or "Mr. Chairperson."
The chair looks at the member and nods, showing that the member has the floor.

or

A member says: "Madame President."
The chair responds: "[the member's name]."

Members may or may not say their names when they try to obtain the floor, as the following example illustrates:

Example
A member says, "Mr. Chairperson, [the member's name]."
The chair responds: "[the member's name]."

A large meeting
A member says, "Madame President," or "Mr. President,
Ms. Hastings of United Industries requests the floor."

The president says, "Ms. Hastings of United Industries has
the floor."

or

The president says, "The president recognizes Ms. Hastings
of United Industries."

According to the rules of parliamentary law, the chair *must*
recognize any member entitled to request the floor. Nevertheless, the chair has the right to ask the member the purpose of the
speech. This can help ensure the smooth flow of debate and the
even exchange of ideas and opinions.

Example
The chair says, "For what purpose does the member request
the floor?"

or

The chair says, "For what purpose does the speaker address
the membership?"

Yielding the floor. Members who have been granted the floor
then make their motions, present any communications, or speak
to the point being debated. Once you are granted the floor, you
have the exclusive right to speak. When you are finished speaking, you *yield* the floor by sitting down again. This signals the
chair that another member can be recognized.

Two or more members claiming the floor. If two or more
members rise to seek the floor at the same time, the member

who first addressed the chair after the floor was yielded has the floor. It is up to the chair to determine who first addressed the chair. A member cannot try to seize the floor by rising before the previous speaker has finished. Such actions are considered out of order.

Interrupting a speaker. In most instances, the person cannot try to interrupt a speaker or cut off debate. An effective chair will not allow such actions, as the following example demonstrates.:

Example
Ms. Doran says, "I think we have to consider selling all our current computers before we buy new hardware."

Mr. Schmidt interrupts, "I move that this meeting be adjourned."

The chair says, "Mr. Schmidt, you are out of order. Ms. Doran has the floor. Take your seat."

There are five instances in which parliamentary law *does* allow a speaker to be interrupted:

1. To call for orders of the day (see page 41)
2. To recognize an objection to the consideration of a question (see page 35)
3. To enter in the minutes a motion to reconsider (see page 29)
4. To allow a point of order (see page 187)
5. To admit a question of privilege that requires immediate action (see page 40)

A person who cuts off another speaker must state the reasons for the interruption, as this example shows.

Example
The speaker says, "Ms. Chairperson, I rise to a point of order [I want to point out that we have not followed parliamentary law]."

If the chair claims the floor. Any member must automatically yield the floor to the chair. This means that if the chair rises to speak before you obtain the floor, you must yield.

Order of speaking. Any member who has had the floor once during a debate may not have it again while the same issue is being debated, if there is any member who has not had a chance to speak yet. Once everyone who desires a turn has had a chance to speak, then members may seek the floor a second time. This rule helps ensure equal representation.

The will of the minority versus rights of the minority. Effective chairs seek to recognize speakers from both sides of an issue during a debate in order to present a balance of opinions. If you are the chair, try to alternate sides by recognizing representatives from one side of the issue and then the other. This is especially crucial when the issue is an explosive one.

ACTIONS BEFORE DEBATE ON A QUESTION

Before any subject is open to debate, three separate actions must be taken:

1. *A motion must be made.* A member must actually make a motion that the assembly consider a particular issue. There are specific words that must be used when a person makes a motion. The member *makes a motion* by *moving* something, as this example shows:

Example
A member says, "I move that we hold our annual convention in San Diego."

2. *A resolution may be made.* If the motion calls for a greater level of formality, the motion can be presented in the form of a *resolution.* Since resolutions are longer and more complex than motions, they are usually prepared in writing before the meeting and the member reads them to the assembly. In these instances, the wording is different, as this example demonstrates:

Example
A member says, "I move the adoption of the following resolution: *Resolved,* that all new employees be approved by a panel comprising at least four members of the executive board."

If the resolution is very long, the member can sign it and pass it to the chair before the meeting instead of reading it to the entire assembly. In these instances, the process is different:

Example
The member says, "I move the assembly approve the resolution relating to [summarizing the matter] which I have sent to the chair."

The chair says, "The resolution offered by [member's name] is as follows: . . ."

3. *The motion must be seconded.* In nearly all instances, after one member makes a motion, another member must second it. Without a second, the motion cannot be discussed by the assembly.

Example
A member says, "I second the motion that we hold our annual convention in San Diego."

or

A member says, "I second the motion."

The following motions do not have to be seconded:

- Call for orders of the day
- Call for the division of the assembly
- Call for separate votes
- Calling a member to order
- Committee recommendations
- Nominations
- Objection to the consideration of a question
- Parliamentary inquiry
- Point of information
- Point of order
- Point of parliamentary inquiry
- Point of personal privilege
- Raising of a question of privilege
- Requests
- Withdrawal of a motion
- A call for orders of the day
- An objection to the consideration of a question

3. *The chair must state the motion.* After steps 1 and 2, the chair must restate the motion:

Example
The chair says, "A motion has been made and seconded that we hold our annual convention in San Diego. The motion is open to debate."

This means that the motion is now *pending,* open to debate. If the members of an organization decide to agree with the motion, it is *adopted* or *carried;* if they decide to vote against it, the motion is *lost* or *rejected.*

CHANGING A MOTION BY THE MOVER

What if the maker of the motion decides it should be debated, but in a different form? Then the person can *modify* the motion. But what if the person who made the motion decides it should not be debated after all? In this instance, the person who made the motion can *withdraw* it. The process is different depending on when the person wants to withdraw the motion. Here are two examples:

Example

Modifying a motion
Mr. Hassad says, "I move that we purchase the used walnut conference table from First National Bank."
Ms. Viceroy says, "I second the motion."
Mr. Hassad says, "Before the chair reads the motion, I would like to modify it to read: 'I move that we purchase the used walnut conference table from First National Bank for a price not to exceed $10,000.'"
The chair says, "Would anyone like to second Mr. Hassad's modified motion?"
Ms. Rivera says, "I second the motion."
The chair says, "The motion to purchase the used walnut conference table from First National Bank for a price not to exceed $10,000 is seconded. It is now open for debate."

Withdrawing a motion before the chair states it
Dr. Ricardo says, "I move that we retain the accounting firm of Calabria and Meyer for the fiscal year 1994–1995."
Ms. Peabody says, "I second the motion."

Dr. Ricardo says, "I would like to withdraw my motion."
Ms. Peabody says, "I withdraw my second."

After the chair states the motion, it can be modified or withdrawn only with the consent of the assembly.

MOTIONS THAT MUST BE IN WRITING

The following motions must be in writing:

1. All main motions (see page 27)
2. All amendments (see page 44)
3. All instructions to committees

DIVISION OF QUESTIONS

When a motion pertaining to a single question has a number of different parts, each of which can stand as a discrete proposition if separated from the others, the parts can be separated and voted on individually. This is achieved by adopting the motion called *division of the question* (or to *divide the question*).

Time. It is usually better to divide the question when it is first proposed, but it can be divided at any point in the debate.

Dividing. The motion to divide must clearly state the way in which the motion is to be divided. If several different proposals are made, they should be voted on in the order in which they were made.

Method. The following example illustrates division of a question:

Example

Ms. Williams: "Resolved, that the company fund all employee travel, reimbursing representatives at the rate of 27¢ per mile."

Mr. Richards: "Madame President, I move that we divide the question so as to consider separately the matter of reimbursement."

Here are the rules that apply to the division of a question:

1. It takes precedence over the main and subsidiary motion to postpone indefinitely.
2. It yields to all subsidiary motions except postpone indefinitely, amend, and limit or extend limits of debate.
3. It can be applied to main motions and amendments if they can be divided.
4. It must be seconded.
5. It cannot be debated.
6. It can be amended.
7. It requires a majority vote to be adopted.
8. It cannot be reconsidered.

3
Motions

MOTIONS AT A GLANCE

HOW TO MAKE A MOTION

First study the correct way to phrase different types of motions:

Motion	What to Say	Second?	Debate?	Amend?	Vote?
Adjourn	"I move that we adjourn."	Yes	No	No	Majority
Adjourn at a future time	"I move to adjourn at [time]." "I move to adjourn sine die." "I move that we adjourn to reconvene at [time]."	Yes	No	No	Majority
Adopt a report	"I move that the report be adopted."	Yes	No	No	Majority
Amend a motion on the floor	"I move to amend by adding . . ." "I move to amend by striking out . . ." "I move to amend by inserting the word . . . before the word . . ."	Yes	Yes	Yes	Majority
Avoid debating an improper matter	"I object to consideration of this motion."	No	No	No	Two-thirds

Motion	What to Say	Second?	Debate?	Amend?	Vote?
Complain about heat, noise, etc.	"I rise to a question of privilege."	No	No	No	None
End debate	"I move the previous question."	Yes	No	No	Two-thirds
Give closer study	"I move to refer the matter to committee."	Yes	Yes	Yes	Majority
Intermission	"I move that we recess for . . ."	Yes	No	Yes	Majority
Introduce business	"I move that . . ."	Yes	Yes	Yes	Majority
Postpone discussion	"I move to postpone discussion until . . ."	Yes	Yes	Yes	Majority
Protest a breach of rules or conduct	"I rise to a point of order."	No	No	No	No vote
Reconsider an action	"I move to reconsider the vote on . . ."	Yes	If debatable	No	Majority
Request information	"Point of information."	No	No	No	No vote
Suspend an issue	"I move to table the motion."	Yes	No	No	Majority

Motion	What to Say	Second?	Debate?	Amend?	Vote?
Suspend the rules	"I move to suspend the rules so that . . ."	Yes	No	No	Two-thirds
Take up a tabled matter	"I move to take from the table . . ."	Yes	No	No	Majority
Verify a vote by having members rise	"I call for a division." "Division!"	No	No	No	No vote
Vote on a chair's ruling	"I appeal from the decision."	Yes	Yes	Yes	Majority

TYPES OF MOTIONS

A *motion* is a proposal for action by the group. Motions are introduced with the words, "I move that _____." Here are two examples:

Example

Ms. Perez: "I move that we establish a task force to examine the merger in greater detail."

or

Mr. Ling: "I move that we adopt the Maxwell proposal."

There are four main types of motions: (1) main motions, (2) secondary motions, (3) incidental motions, and (4) privileged motions. Each type of motion accomplishes a different action and is treated differently. Let's look at each type of motion, starting with the most common one, the main motion.

Main Motions

A *main motion* introduces a new item of business. Only one main motion can be considered at a time. Don't be misled by the name—main motions are the lowest ranking motions. They are superseded by higher ranking motions, such as subsidiary motions, privileged motions, and incidental motions.

How do you make a main motion?

1. The member rises and addresses the chair. The member uses the chair's correct title and preferred form of address.

Example
A member says, "Madame Chair."

          or

A member says, "Mr. President."

2. The chair recognizes the member.

Example
The chair says, "The chair recognizes Jay Harris."

3. The member makes the motion.

Example
A member says, "I move that we recommend the Bradley Group be retained for this project."

4. Another member seconds the motion.

Example
A member says, "Madame Chairperson, I second the motion."

5. The chair repeats the motion.

Example
A member says, "A motion has been made that we recommend the Bradley Group be retained for this project."

6. The chair calls for discussion on the motion.

Example
The chair says, "The motion to recommend the Bradley Group be retained for this project has been seconded. It is now open to discussion."

7. After the debate is concluded, the chair puts the motion to a vote.

Example
The chair says, "As many are in favor [as the question may be] say aye. As many are in opposition [as the question may be] say no."

or

"It has been moved and seconded that [motion]. Those in favor of the adoption raise their right hands [pause for yes vote]. Those opposed do the same."

or

"You've heard the resolution read. Those in favor of its adoption raise their right hands [pause for yes vote]. Those opposed do the same."

8. The chair announces the result of the vote.

Example
The chair says, "The motion is carried—the resolution is adopted."

or

"The ayes have it—the resolution is adopted."

What can you do to a main motion?
A main motion can be:

- Seconded
- Voted for
- Postponed
- Referred to a committee
- Objected to
- Divided
- Rescinded (after approval)
- Debated
- Voted against
- Amended
- Laid on the table
- Withdrawn
- Reconsidered
- Amended (after adoption)
- Renewed (if rejected)

To help you remember how main motions work, memorize this acronym: SDAMR.

S	*S*econdable
D	*D*ebatable
A	*A*mendable
M	*M*ajority vote
R	*R*econsiderable

Main motions and resolutions
Resolutions are main motions but differ in their format from other such motions. Because resolutions are usually expressions

of policy, principal, sentiment, or feeling, they tend to have a preamble. Because of their length and complexity, resolutions should always be presented in writing. Nonetheless, because resolutions are main motions, they are presented in the same way.

All resolutions are main motions, but not all main motions are resolutions. Resolution types are as follows:

- Without a preamble
- With a preamble of one "Whereas"
- With a preamble of more than one "Whereas"
- With one "Resolved"
- With more than one "Resolved"
- With any combination of the above

Subsidiary Motions

Subsidiary (secondary) motions are motions applied to other motions to help the members dispose of main motions. Here are the six subsidiary motions:

- Lay on the table
- Previous question
- Postpone to a certain time
- Commit or refer
- Amend
- Postpone

Qualities of Subsidiary Motions
1. They never stand alone. A *subsidiary* motion is always applied to another motion.
2. They always change the status of the other motion by modifying it in some way.
3. They can be applied to any main motion and to some subsidiary motions.
4. They are treated in a specific order. (See page 33.)

When to Use Subsidiary Motions

1. *Lay on the table to set aside a motion.* If the members wish to set aside a motion without establishing a time for the debate to resume, they can use the subsidiary motion "lay on the table." This motion enables members to resume the discussion at any point with a majority vote. Here is the way the motion is made:

Example
A member says, "I move that the motion be laid on the table."

2. *Move the previous question to limit discussion.* If members wish to bring a motion to an immediate vote, they can make a motion to move the previous question. This closes debate and forces members to consider the matter at once. A sample format follows:

Example
A member says, "I move the previous question."

or

A member says, "I demand the previous question."

3. *Postpone a main motion to a certain time when time is tight.* If the members want to continue to think about a motion but the debate has run too long, a member can use the subsidiary motion to postpone to move consideration of the question to a later time in the meeting. The motion might also be made as "postpone to a certain time" or "postpone definitely." The motion is made as follows:

Example
A member says, "I move that the motion be postponed until [a specific time] and then made a special order."

or

A member says, "I move to postpone the question to the next meeting."

4. *Refer or commit to take a closer look at an issue.* What if the motion needs fine tuning, but the assembly lacks the time? What if the assembly needs more information to make an informed decision? In these instances, the subsidiary motion to commit or to refer allows the members to send the motion to a committee for further study or redrafting. Here is how you make this motion:

Example
A member says, "I move to refer the motion to the finance committee for further study."

or

A member says, "I move that the motion be referred to a committee of seven members to be elected by the membership."

5. *Amend a main motion to change it.* If a member makes a motion that is unclear or too broad, it can be clarified or narrowed by being *amended.* The subsidiary motion to amend allows members to target motions and make them more precise and thus more likely to accomplish their intended goal. You make this motion as follows:

Example
A member says, "I move to amend the motion by crossing out the last paragraph."

or

A member says, "I move to substitute for the pending motion the following motion . . ."

or

A member says, "I move to amend the motion by adding . . ."

or

A member says, "I move to amend the motion by inserting the word . . . before the word . . ."

6. *Postpone a main motion to prevent embarrassment.* If a member has brought a main motion that could cause people to become embarrassed or uncomfortable, members would not want to bring it to a vote. A member could use a subsidiary motion, to postpone indefinitely, to remove the motion from the assembly. A sample form follows:

Example
A member says, "I move that the motion be postponed indefinitely."

Order of Precedence

As mentioned before, subsidiary motions fit into an order of precedence; some subsidiary motions take precedence over other subsidiary motions. A subsidiary motion has precedence over a main motion, which means that it must be decided before the members can act on the main motion. Here are the six subsidiary motions listed in order of precedence:

1. Lay on the table
2. Previous question
3. Postpone to a certain time
4. Commit or refer
5. Amend
6. Postpone

You can make any of these subsidiary motions when a lower order motion is on the floor. But you cannot make a subsidiary motion if a higher order one is being considered.

Applying Subsidiary Motions

Subsidiary motions are applied to main motions most of the time, but they can be applied to other subsidiary motions under certain circumstances.

- A motion for the previous question can be applied to a motion to postpone without affecting the main motion.
- Motions to postpone to a certain day, to commit, and to amend can themselves be amended.
- The motion to amend a specific portion of the minutes can be laid on the table without all the minutes being tabled.

As you will see, subsidiary motions yield to privileged and incidental motions (pages 34, 38).

Incidental Motions

An *incidental motion* comes from another motion, which means that it always relates directly to the business on the floor. Members make incidental motions as a result of another pending motion, or an item of business that:

- They wish to propose
- Has been made but not stated by the chair
- Is pending

Unlike subsidiary motions, incidental motions do not pertain to a main motion over the entire time it is being debated.

Qualities of Incidental Motions

1. Incidental motions take precedence over all other motions except privileged ones.

2. Usually, they must be decided before the meeting can continue.
3. They must be decided before other motions.
4. They cannot be amended.
5. Except for appeal, they cannot be debated.

When to Use Incidental Motions

1. *Appeals.* These are used to appeal the chair's ruling on an issue. The appeal forces the chair to submit the matter to a vote by the membership. If the vote is a tie, the chair's decision stands. One member makes a motion to appeal, another member seconds the motion, and the chair calls for a vote, as shown in the following example:

> **Example**
> **A member says, "I appeal the chair's decision."**
> **Another member says, "I second the motion."**
> **The chair says, "Shall the chair's decision stand as the judgment of the organization?"**

Appeals:

- Yield to privileged questions.
- Cannot be amended.
- Cannot be debated when they pertain to behavior or the order of business. If the issue can be debated, every member can speak only once.
- Allow the president to speak without leaving the chair.

2. *Objections to the consideration of a question.* What happens if a member does not want the assembly to debate a question because it is off the topic or is likely to cause trouble? After the motion has been introduced, the member can make a motion to object to the consideration of a question. This must be done *before* the debate has begun. After the motion to object to the

consideration of a question has been made, the assembly votes on it. The motion must pass by a two-thirds majority, or the discussion is dropped. The following example shows how the motion is made:

Example
A member says, "I object to the considerations of the question."
The chair says, "Shall the question be discussed?"

or

The chair says, "Shall the question be considered?"

An objection to the consideration of a question:

- Cannot be debated
- Cannot be amended
- Cannot have any subsidiary motion applied to it

→ **TROUBLESHOOTING** **Remember: An objection to the consideration of the question is not intended to cut off debate—there are other motions for that purpose. Instead, it is intended to prevent discussion of a pointless or potentially inflammatory topic.**

3. *Reading papers.* All members have the right to request that papers be read before the assembly. However, this motion should be used only to gather information, not to delay debate or waste time. This is the only information that members have a right to request be read to the assembly.

A motion to read papers:

- Cannot be debated
- Cannot be amended

4. *Withdrawing a motion.* What if you make a motion and then change your mind about it? In these instances, you can withdraw the motion, effectively removing it from consideration. It is as though the original motion had never been made. If

another member objects, however, the chair will have to ask for a vote on the issue.

A motion to withdraw:

- Cannot be debated
- Cannot be amended

There are a number of other requests and inquiries that members can make, as follows:

- *Parliamentary inquiry:* A member can request the chair's ruling on a matter of parliamentary procedure. This is answered by the chair.
- *Point of information:* A member can ask for information about the matter being debated. The request must be answered by the chair.
- *Request to be excused from a duty:* The request can be granted only by the membership.
- *Request for any other privilege:* The request can be granted only by the membership.

5. *Suspending the rules.* This motion is used when the assembly wants to discuss an issue in a way that violates standing rules or rules or order. The organization's constitution or bylaws are *not* involved—they *cannot* be suspended under any circumstances. A member can make a motion to suspend the rules to allow the discussion. A two-thirds vote is required. The motion is made as follows:

Example
A member says, "I move to suspend the rules that interfere with [the specific matter at hand]."

A motion to suspend the rules:

- Cannot be debated
- Cannot be amended

Order of Precedence

Incidental motions are in order only when they are truly incidental to another motion being considered by the assembly. Then these motions take precedence over any other motions on the floor.

1. *Ranking:* Unlike other motions, incidental motions *do not* have rank; therefore, they cannot be assigned precedence over each other.
2. *Right of way:* Incidental motions have precedence over main motions. Further, making an appeal, objections to the consideration of a question, reading papers, withdrawing a motion, and suspending the rules yield to privileged motions.

→ **TROUBLESHOOTING   While it is true that incidental motions always take precedence over main motions, the incidental motion is valid only when it is truly incidental—if it is made at the correct point in the debate.**

Privileged Motions

Privileged motions are different from subsidiary and incidental motions because they do not deal with business on the floor. Rather, they have to do with special matters of pressing importance. They are also called *privileged questions* and should not be confused with questions of privilege (page 40). Here are the four privileged motions:

- Fixing the time to adjourn
- Adjourning
- Questions of privilege
- Orders of the day

Qualities of Privileged Motions

1. Privileged motions take precedence over all other motions.
2. Privileged motions can interrupt any business, without discussion or debate.
3. Like subsidiary motions, however, privileged motions do not fit into an order of precedence.

When to Use Privileged Motions

1. *Fixing the time to adjourn:* There may be times during a debate when members need to set the date for the next meeting. In these instances, any member can fix the time to adjourn. This can be done even during a debate. As the highest ranking of the privileged motions, this motion is in order even if the assembly has voted to adjourn (as long as the chair has not announced the result of the adjournment vote).

- The motion cannot be debated.
- The motion can be amended by changing the time.
- When introduced as a main motion, it can be debated and suppressed as with any other main motion.

Example
A member says, "That when this assembly adjourns, it adjourns to meet at _____ time."

2. *Adjourning:* Any member can call for an adjournment—even during a debate—as long as a time for the next meeting has already been established. You cannot make a motion to adjourn if someone else has the floor, however. If the motion to adjourn is qualified with another privileged motion, it loses its standing as a privileged motion and becomes another main motion. As a result, a privileged motion to adjourn cannot:

- Be debated.
- Be amended.
- Be reconsidered.
- Have a privileged motion applied to it.

A motion to adjourn is useful when it is necessary to take a short break in the debate, or during an election when the tellers are busy counting the ballots. It gives members a chance to take a break or officers an opportunity to complete some necessary executive business. To take a short break, or *recess,* a member can make the following motion:

> **Example**
> **A member says, "I move that we adjourn to meet at the call of the chair."**

An assembly is free to approve or to deny a motion to adjourn, but members can make the motion again if it is denied. How does the motion to adjourn affect business on the floor?

- Business left unfinished at the end of a meeting becomes the first order of business at the next meeting. The business is considered as though there had not been a break.
- Business left unfinished at the end of a session is taken up at the next session. However, if the members are elected for a specific term, such as a year, any unfinished business is dropped at the end of the term, because the members have rotated offices.
- Business left unfinished at the end of a yearly meeting is dropped. Nevertheless, it can be reintroduced at the next session as if it had never been considered by the organization.

3. *Raise a question of privilege to make an urgent request about a person's rights:* If there is something wrong with

the physical surroundings (e.g., faulty air conditioning or a noisy heating system) or a situation arises that affects the rights of the entire assembly (e.g., someone raises a confidential organizational matter before a guest), any individual member can interrupt the motion under consideration to bring the matter to the attention of the chair. If the situation cannot be resolved informally (e.g., by turning down the air conditioning), the chair then rules on whether the matter is a question of privilege and should be considered before business is resumed.

4. *Call for orders of the day to enforce the schedule:* If the agenda is not being followed, or a specific question is supposed to be debated at a certain time and has not been taken up, an individual member can *call for the orders of the day*. This requires that the agenda be followed, unless the assembly decides by a two-thirds vote to set aside the orders of the day.

Order of Precedence

As mentioned before, privileged motions fit into an order of precedence. This means that some privileged motions take precedence over other subsidiary motions. Here is the order of precedence:

1. Fixing the time to adjourn
2. Adjourning
3. Questions of privilege
4. Orders of the day

UNDERSTANDING MOTIONS

1. *Ranking.* Parliamentary motions have rank. Learn which motions take precedence over others. Main motions, for instance, rank lowest. This means that they yield to all subsidiary, privileged, and pertinent incidental motions.

2. *Situations.* Each motion applies to a specific situation. Main motions, for example, cannot be applied to any other motions. Most subsidiary, privileged, and incidental motions can be applied to main motions.

3. *Timing.* Only certain motions can be on the floor at the same time.

4. *Seconding.* Remember that some motions need a second; others do not. The following motions do *not* require a second:

- Call for orders of the day
- Call for the division of the assembly
- Call for separate votes
- Calling a member to order
- Committee recommendations
- Nominations
- Objection to the consideration of a question
- Parliamentary inquiry
- Point of information
- Point of order
- Point of parliamentary inquiry
- Point of personal privilege
- Raise of a question of privilege
- Requests
- Withdrawal of a motion

5. *Debatable.* Remember that some motions can be debated; others cannot be.

6. *Amendable.* Remember that some motions can be amended; others cannot be.

7. *Votes.* How many votes are needed for a motion to pass?

8. *Reconsideration.* Can the motion be reconsidered?

MANIPULATING MOTIONS

There is an art to using parliamentary procedure to gain your objectives. At meetings, you can apply specific tactics to ensure either the passage or the defeat of motions and resolutions. The following methods can help you accomplish your purpose.

To help DEFEAT a motion	*To help PASS a motion*
Do not second the motion. Remain silent.	Second the motion.
Rise and speak against the motion.	Rise and speak for the motion.
Vote against the motion.	Vote for the motion.
Move to postpone the motion indefinitely to kill it outright.	Vote against indefinite postponement to rescue the motion.
Amend the motion to complicate or encumber it.	Defeat adverse amendments and propose useful ones.
Move to refer the motion to committee to prolong it.	Vote against referring it to committee.
Move to postpone the motion to the next meeting.	Vote against postponement and pass the motion now.
Move the question to close off discussion of the motion's good points.	Defeat the previous question so you can more fully discuss the motion's good points.
Move to table the motion.	Vote against tabling it.
Move to take a recess so you can find additional votes.	Defeat the motion to recess so opponents cannot get votes.

If the motion passes, move to reconsider it.	Defeat attempts to reconsider your motion.
Move to adjourn.	Defeat adjournment.
Pack the house with your voting supporters.	Pack the house with your voting supporters.
Abide by the result to maintain the organization's integrity.	Abide by the result to maintain the organization's integrity.

A final note. Remember that the voters decide the question. To manipulate a motion in your favor, have your voters at the meeting and urge them to stay until the end. Defend and oppose motions with all your eloquence and skill; but, above all, abide by the final result. This will safeguard the organization's unity, integrity, and dignity.

AMENDMENTS

What is an amendment? An amendment is a change made to a motion.

What is its purpose? The primary purpose of an amendment is to improve and perfect a motion, most often a main motion, in an attempt to make it more acceptable to an assembly.

How do amendments work? Chairs can ask that amendments be submitted in writing. Once a motion has been moved, seconded, and repeated by the chair, you do not need the permission of the mover to amend the motion because it then belongs to the assembly. When the words of an amendment have been adopted, these same words cannot be changed unless the place or wording is so changed as to constitute a new proposition.

How many kinds of amendments are there? There are two kinds of amendments: *primary* and *secondary*. Let's take a look at each.

1. *Primary (first-degree) amendments:*
   • Must be germane to the motion to which they are applied.
   • Can be amended.
2. *Secondary (second-degree) amendments:*
   • Seek to change a primary amendment to which they must be germane.
   • Do not apply directly to the main motion.
   • Cannot be amended.

How do you amend a motion? There are five main ways of amending a motion:

1. *Add word(s) at the end of the motion.*

   Example
   Ms. Margoshes says, "I move that the organization purchase a new radio."
   Mr. Ricco says, "I amend the motion to read: The organization should purchase a new radio *at a cost not to exceed $150.*"

2. *Insert word(s) at any place in the motion.* For the sake of logic, words inserted in an amendment should be consecutive, not scattered.

   Example
   Mr. Washington says, "I move that the company purchase a new car."
   Ms. DiPinto says, "I amend the motion to read, The company should purchase a new [brand name] car."

3. *Strike out word(s).*

   Example
   Ms. Elleniski says, "I move that the company purchase a new desk and computer for the Fort Worth office."
   Mr. Poskanzer says, "I amend the motion to strike out words 'and computer' in the motion."

4. *Strike out word(s) and add others.*

   Example
   Ms. Hernandez says, "I move that we serve a turkey dinner at the opening meeting."
   Mr. Smyth says, "I amend the motion to strike out word 'turkey' and insert 'roast beef.'"

5. *Substitute another motion, replacing the pending motion in its entirety with another motion related to the same subject.*

   Example
   Mr. Villas says, "I move that we take a trip to Atlantic City for next year's annual holiday social affair."
   Ms. Accardi says, "I want to substitute the following motion: 'that in lieu of our annual holiday social affair we hold a holiday party for the needy children of our neighborhood.'"

Two amendments of the same degree cannot be considered at the same time. This means that you cannot have two primary or two secondary amendments on a motion at the same time.

How do you make an amendment? Always remember that an amendment:

• Must pertain to the motion on the floor.
• Must be seconded.

- Can be debated when the motion to which it is applied can be debated.
- Requires a majority vote to be adopted.
- Can be reconsidered.
- Is limited in number; no more than two can be pending at the same time to a motion.
- May be hostile but not negative. For example, the word *praise* can be changed to *reprimand,* but the word *praise* cannot be changed to *not praise*.

   Amendments that are simple and accepted by the membership may be adopted by unanimous consent without going through the formal amending process.

4

Committees

Experienced parliamentarians recognize that most organizations are too big and their meetings too brief to do more than plan for work to be done. As the amount of work and the pace of life increase as we approach the 21st century, this problem will intensify. How can organizations get through all their work in a timely, equitable manner?

WHAT IS A COMMITTEE?

Most large organizations delegate their work to *committees*. According to parliamentary law:

a *committee* is a group of one or more persons, elected or appointed to consider or to take action on a specific matter.

Unlike a board, a committee is not strictly defined as a form of assembly. Do not be misled by this definition into thinking that a committee is always small. As you will read, some committees can be very large.

The word *committee* implies that as a body it cannot act apart from the larger group. A committee must have special directions from the assembly to take action on its own. Also, a committee does not have regularly scheduled meetings.

ADVANTAGES OF COMMITTEES

Even in small organizations, dividing tasks and assigning them to specific committees makes a lot of sense. Committees can save time and have a number of advantages:

1. *Size*

- A small number of people can arrange meetings more easily than a larger group. It's much easier to call them together, especially through electronic means such as E-mail and fax.
- A small group of peple can deliberate more efficiently than a larger group. As a result, they can work more quickly than a large, often unwieldy organization.

2. *Informal procedure*

- In small committee meetings (12 persons or less), the formality of large assemblies is unnecessary. Therefore, the rules governing such meetings are different from the rules governing larger groups.
- The chair of a committee can enter into discussion without rising or leaving the chair.
- The chair of a committee is allowed to make motions and vote on all questions, actions that are not allowed in a general assembly.
- In a committee setting, members are not required to obtain the floor before making motions and speaking. This means that they do not have to rise and be recognized.
- Members can speak as long and as often as they wish.
- Motions to close or limit debate are not allowed.
- Questions can be raised while discussion is going on.
- Informal discussion is allowed if there is no motion pending on the floor.

- Motions do not have to be seconded.
- When all committee members understand a proposal, a vote may be taken without a formal motion being introduced.

  3. *Fewer distractions*

- Committees can work more quietly and efficiently.
- Members save time by streamlining parliamentary procedure.

  4. *Deliberations*

- Committees can make better use of experts and consultants since they are more flexible about time and scheduling.

  5. *Privacy*

- Because committees are smaller than the entire organization, they are better equipped to handle delicate, troublesome, and embarrassing questions.
- Committees are often used for such matters as raises, promotions, and discipline in business, and for selection of officers and honors in honorary organizations.

  6. *Expediency.* The judicious appointment of committees can help keep delicate, troublesome, and time-consuming debates out of the general meeting. If the committees are balanced and properly constituted with representatives of all interests, matters that might get very unplesant in a general meeting can be handled expeditiously in a committee.

MAKING COMMITTEES MEANINGFUL

Unfortunately, committees are often misused. They may become burial grounds for unpleasant issues, a method of rewarding members and distributing titles to friends, or a device for giving everyone something to do. Occasionally, they are even used to placate chronic troublemakers. How can you make sure that the committees in your organization serve a real purpose?

1. *Useful work:* No committee should be appointed unless it is needed. Members of a committee that has no real work will soon recognize this fact and lost interest in the committee. Busy work serves no one's best interests.
2. *Timely agenda:* Most pepole work better when they know that their work must be completed by a specific date. The report of the committee should be placed on the agenda so that members know that the end date is real and will be followed.
3. *Membership:* Try to select people who work together well. This is especially crucial if the committee is charged with a delicate task.

TYPES OF COMMITTEES

A committee is a miniature assembly that meets to transact business. What do you need for a committee? Consider the following:

Committee Checklist
- Number of committee members
- Method of selecting members
- Specific task
- Where the committee will meet
- How often the committee will meet
- The date the committee report is due

There are three main kinds of committees: (1) *standing committees,* committees that have a continued existence; (2) *special committees* (also called *select* or *ad hoc* committees), which are appointed for a particular purpose and cease to exist once that purpose has been served; and (3) *committees of the whole,* made up of the entire assembly. There are also two simpler types of committees of the whole—*quasi committee of the whole* and *informal consideration of a question.* Let's take a look at each type of committee in detail.

1. *Standing committees*

- *Method of selection:* It is specified by the organization's by-laws. A standing committee also can be created by a resolution passed by a two-thirds majority vote.
- *Term of office:* Because standing committees remain in existence permanently, members serve extended terms. In most cases, these terms are the same as those served by officers in the organization. Therefore, new members of standing committees are usually appointed when new officers are elected to head the organization.
- *Function:* Standing committees handle routine duties that need to be carried out on a regular basis. These may include publishing a newsletter, fundraising, screening new members, or awarding honors.
- *Workings:* A standing committee reports to the assembly, not to the board of directors, unless the bylaws state otherwise.

2. *Special (select or ad hoc) committees*

- *Method of selection:* This is determined in the bylaws.
- *Term of office:* Special committees are disbanded when the particular task is completed. They may be re-created at a later date, however, when the task once again presents itself. For example, an organization may need to reconsider its staffing and technological needs periodically.
- *Function:* These committees are established to accomplish a particular task. For example, a special committee may be created to investigate the possibility of purchasing state-of-the-art computer equipment or updating existing hardware.

- *Workings:* A special committee is devoted to a particular task and should not be established if its duties are covered by a standing committee.

3. *Committees of the whole.* How can there be a committee of the entire assembly? Why would the entire assembly want to consider an issue as a committee? A committee of the whole is a very useful provision of parliamentary law, one that is used extensively in legislative bodies. It works as follows:

- *Method of selection:* When an assembly wants to debate a subject but not refer it to committee, or when the information is not yet fully understood and codified, the assembly can create a committee of the whole. To create a committee of the whole, a member should make a motion to commit, in the following form:

    Example
    A member says, "That the assembly does now resolve itself into a committee of the whole, to take under consideration [the specific resolution or subject].

    or

    "I move to go into a committee of the whole to consider the pending question."

The motion needs a second. If the motion is carried, the chair immediately calls another member to the chair and takes his or her place as a member of the committee. In large assemblies, the clerk also vacates his or her seat and the assistant clerk assumes it.

- *Term of office:* Committees of the whole, like special committees, are disbanded when the particular task is completed. They may be re-created at a later date, however, when the task once again presents itself.

- *Function:* A committee of the whole allows members to consider the matter with the freedom of a committee. For example, the chair can participate in the debate, make motions, and vote on all questions, actions not allowed in a general assembly. A committee of the whole can only make the following motions: (1) to amend and (2) to adopt.
- *Workings:* A committee of the whole cannot alter the resolution it is debating. If there is no limit to debate, members can speak to an issue as long as they want. To close or limit debate, a member of the assembly has to make a motion.

Example
A member says, "I make a motion that the committee rise and report."

The motion to *rise and report* is the same as a motion to adjourn. It cannot be debated. Members immediately vote on the motion; if it passes, the chair resumes his or her place, and the chair of the committee returns to the floor. The chair of the committee then rises and says:

Example
The chair says, "I move that the committee rise."

or

The chair says, "As chair of the committee of the whole, I report that the committee has gone through the business referred to it, and I am ready to make a report when the assembly is ready to receive it."

4. *Quasi committee of the whole*

- *Method of selection:* This is a streamlined version of the committee of the whole, convenient for medium-sized assemblies (50–100 members).
- *Term of office:* Quasi committees of the whole, like special

committees, are disbanded when the particular task is completed. They may be re-created at a later date, however, when the task once again presents itself.

- *Function:* Like a committee of the whole, a quasi committee of the whole allows members to consider the matter with the freedom of a committee.
- *Workings:* Technically, this is not actually a committee but is simply the assembly acting as a committee of the whole. The results of all votes are given to the entire assembly for final consideration, as with the committee of the whole. All members are allowed to speak as often as they like and for as long as they like. The difference lies in the type of motions allowed. If any motion other than an amendment is accepted, the committee is automatically over. Also, in a quasi committee of the whole, the chair retains his or her position as the presiding officer of the assembly.

To create a quasi committee of the whole, a member says,

Example
A member says, "I move that the resolution be considered in quasi committee of the whole."

The motion must have a second. To bring the committee to an end, use this format:

Example
The chair says, "The assembly, acting as if in a committee of the whole, has had under consideration [the task] and has made the following amendments [specific amendments]. The question is on the adoption of the amendments."

5. *Informal consideration of a question*

- *Method of selection:* This is a still further simplified version of the quasi committee of the whole.

- *Term of office:* Like a quasi committee of the whole, this committee is disbanded when the particular task is completed. It may be re-created at a later date, however, when the task once again presents itself.
- *Function:* Increasingly, many assemblies consider certain issues informally rather than forming a committee of the whole. This saves time.
- *Workings:* Technically, this is not a true committee, but the assembly acting as a committee of the whole. The chair stays seated, and every member can speak as often and as long as desired. The clerk should keep a record of what transpires, but the record should not be entered into the minutes because it is only for temporary use. While acting informally, the entire group can amend and adopt resolutions, and without further motion the chair can announce:

Example
The chair says that, "The assembly, acting informally, has considered [the subject] and has made certain amendments, which the chair will report at this time."

At that point, the matter comes before the assembly as if reported by a committee. The chair's report becomes part of the regular minutes.

When different committees are voted on, the voting must follow this order:

1. Committee of the whole
2. Standing committee
3. Special (select or ad hoc) committee

FORMING COMMITTEES

To form a committee, follow these steps:

1. *Make a motion.* A motion must be made to refer a matter to a committee:

Example
A member says, "I move to refer the matter [or subject] to a committee."

2. *Appoint a chair.* The next step in creating a committee is naming someone to head it. The president of the assembly normally appoints the committee chair. If the assembly or the president has not elected a chair, the committee, once formed, has the authority to name or elect a new chair.

The responsibilities of the committee chair are to:

- Understand the committee's task.
- Explain the committee's goals to members.
- Guide—not direct—the discussion.
- Coordinate suggestions.
- Make sure all statements are clearly understood.
- Keep an open mind.

3. *Appoint committee members.* The assembly or chair then appoints members to the committee. The chair makes a motion to appoint members. The motion is phrased as follows:

Example
The chair says, "Of how many shall the committee consist?"

- If the committee is a select one and the motion does not describe how it shall be appointed, nor is the matter included in the organization's bylaws, then the chair asks how the committee shall be appointed.

- In some instances, the chair appoints members; at other times, the members are nominated by the chair of members of the organization.
- In most cases, no member can nominate more than one person unless this rule is set aside by common consent.
- Nominees are all voted on together unless more members are nominated than are needed. Then, they are voted on individually.
- Usually, one of the members is appointed clerk or secretary at this time. This allows the committee to begin its business more quickly, as the clerk sends out the call for the meeting.

How many people should serve on a committee? The number of people on a committee depends on the task the committee has been assigned.

- *Action committees:* In general, when the committee has to decide on an action, such as purchasing land or arranging for a special meeting, the number of members involved should be small. Further, unless the action is highly controversial, all members should support the action. Those who do not should decline the nomination and excuse themselves from serving.
- *Investigation committees:* When the committee is charged with an investigative or deliberative mission, it is crucial that all interests be fully represented to ensure that the rights of both the minority and the majority are protected. Such representation will also help cut down on divisiveness later on, when the committee delivers its report to the entire assembly.

Keep in mind, however, that committee size often influences the committee's impact. Although a large committee is undeniably harder to maneuver than a small one, its report is usually more persuasive because of the number of members involved.

This factor may influence people who are trying to block or to support specific issues.

4. *Give the committee its task.* The chair formally writes out the task and gives it to the committee. This paper or papers should not be written on any further.

5. *Call the meetings.* The chair then calls the committee together for the first time. If there is a quorum, the chair either reads or has read the committee's charge. Any two committee members can call a meeting to transact business if the chair is absent or refuses to call a meeting. Then the members discuss the resolution and begin their work.

6. *Notify ex-officio members.* These members are part of the committee by virtue of holding some other office. The president of the organization is usually an ex-officio member of all committees, unless otherwise stated in the bylaws of the organization. Ex-officio members have all the privileges but none of the obligations of membership. Such membership allows the president (and other officers covered under this regulation) to participate in a committee, but does not mandate it. The president's rights as an ex-officio member of a committee are as follows:

- Shares the same rights as any other committee member.
- Can make motions and vote.
- Is not counted in determining a quorum.
- Is not obligated to attend meetings.

7. *Report to the chair.* When the committee has completed its work, any committee member makes a motion for the committee to report to the chair of the assembly. This is called a *motion to rise* and is the same as a motion to adjourn. After the committee makes its report, its work is finished, and the committee is disbanded.

INITIAL MEETINGS

What happens when a committee meets for the first time? Following are two factors you must consider at once: a quorum and minutes.

Quorum. As with all meetings, there has to be a *quorum*. In a committee, a quorum is a majority of members, unless the number has been fixed in the bylaws or the specific resolution that created the committee. The meeting is not considered legal unless all members have been notified. In most instances, this task falls to the clerk of the organization as a whole. For subsequent meetings, the committee clerk will notify all members.

Minutes. It is very important that the secretary or clerk take accurate, detailed minutes of all committee meetings, for these minutes will be used later as the source for the committee report. Included in the minutes should be a record of the steps the committee took to arrive at its decision. It is also advisable to include a record of the opinions members expressed, the information they gathered, and the actions they took. The best minutes help make the best committee reports. Minutes remain the property of the committee and can be read only by committee members.

Use the following checklist to organize your initial committee meeting:

Initial Committee Meeting Checklist
✓ List of committee members
✓ Copy of the resolution referred to committee
✓ Statement of the committee's task; if available, special instructions
✓ Statement of the committee's powers
✓ Copies of any pertinent rules

✓ Copies of any relevant correspondence
✓ Copies of any previous decisions relevant to the issue
✓ Information about the report format
✓ Date the report is due to the membership

PREPARING AND UTILIZING COMMITTEE REPORTS

To fulfill its mission, a committee must report to the assembly, describing its findings and including any resolutions. The entire committee submits a report. About 90 percent of the time, a committee's report is accepted by the assembly and decides what course of action the assembly will take on an issue. The minority may submit its views in writing, but a minority report can be acted on only when the committee votes to substitute one for the majority report.

What can you expect to find in a committee report? Committee reports include the following:

• Identification of the committee submitting it
• Statement of the resolution given to the committee
• Summary of the methods of investigation the committee used
• Summary of the information the committee gathered
• Summary of the work accomplished
• Committee findings
• Committee recommendations

Steps in the writing process. As with nearly all group writing, a committee report is amassed in stages, as all members contribute their opinions, phrases, and suggestions. This can be a cumbersome and time-consuming process. We suggest these steps to streamline the process:

• *Select one writer.* To expedite the actual composition, have one committee member write the entire first draft. Choose a person who not only writes well but also is well respected by the committee and represents the majority opinion. The report is written in the first person plural ("We report," not "I report").

- *Utilize computer technology.* We recommend using a high-quality word-processing program. Be sure the software is compatible with that used by the clerk, for this will make revisions much easier. Also try to use the same operating system to avoid having to make disk conversions. Bring both disk and hard copy to meetings.

- *Share the report.* The draft is reproduced and a copy is given to every member. Allow ample time for members to study the draft at home. Every committee member marks the draft with specific suggestions, emendations, and corrections.

- *Revise as a group.* At a specified meeting, the committee chair reads the draft aloud, one paragraph at a time. The chair should pause after each paragraph and say, "Are there any amendments any member would like to make here?" The members discuss proposed changes, and the clerk then makes the changes on his or her copy. This is most easily accomplished by having the clerk make the changes directly on line.

- *Reflect the majority voice.* As the committee prepares its report, it should be careful to include the combined majority voice of the entire committee. This is in keeping with the aim of parliamentary procedure: to reflect the voice of the majority while protecting the rights of the minority. What happens when a minority does not agree with the majority? In these instances, the minority can file its own report.

- *Adopt the report.* After the whole report has been read and discussed, the committee can adopt it at once if everyone is satisfied. If there have been many changes, the committee can have the clerk prepare a clean copy for the committee to reconsider. If there is widespread dissatisfaction, the committee can reject the entire report, request that a new one be prepared in its place, and then repeat the process.

Form of Committee Reports

Committee reports usually follow this form:

Example

For standing committees
> **Report of the [name of the committee]**
> The committee on [specific committee charge] respectfully reports that . . . [the text of the report].
>> **Respectfully submitted,**
>> **[Chair of the Committee]**

or

For special or select committees
> **Report of the [name of the committee]**
> The committee to which was referred [specific committee charge], having considered the matter, respectfully reports . . . [the text of the report].
>> **Respectfully submitted,**
>> **[Chair of the Committee]**

Signing the report. Reports are usually signed only by the committee chair. However, if the matter is very important, every committee member who agrees with the report should sign it.

Minority Reports

Minority reports express the views of those committee members who disagree with the committee report. Some guidelines for minority reports follow.

1. *A privilege, not a right.* A minority report is a privilege, not a right. Appointing a committee in the first place implies that the assembly is primarily interested in the findings of the majority of committee members, not the minority. Check your bylaws: A minority report is usually allowed by the assembly when permission is requested.

2. *Rights of the minority.* When committee members debate their report, any member of the committee who does not agree with the majority has the right to speak individually in opposition. In addition, the minority has the right to recommend the following options with regard to the report:

- Rejection of the resolution
- Amendment of the resolution
- Adoption of some other suitable motion to dispose of the resolution appropriately
- Acceptance of part of the report

3. *Adding a statement to the report.* If a written committee report is signed by everyone on the committee who agrees, and a committee member agrees with the entire report except for one or more items, the member can add a statement to the report in which the member explains his or her agreement with the report except the part so specified and then signs the statement. This is done last, after everyone in agreement has signed the report.

4. *Confidentiality guaranteed.* Whatever is said in committee cannot be repeated outside the confines of the meeting. No one can make reference to what occurred during committee deliberations unless it is by report of the committee or by general consent.

5. *Format.* A minority report may take the following form:

Example
   Report of the [name of the committee]
The undersigned, a minority of the members of the [name of the committee] appointed to [task of the committee] to which we were referred, not agreeing with the majority, desire to express their views in the case . . . [text of the report].
   Respectfully submitted,
   [Minority members]

Whether the views of the minority are presented formally or not, any member can move at a regular meeting of the entire assembly that the resolutions proposed by the committee be amended, that they be postponed indefinitely, or that some other appropriate action be taken.

Delivering the Report

After the report is completed and signed, it is routed as follows:

- The committee chair or committee member appointed for this purpose brings the report to a regular meeting of the entire assembly.
- This speaker explains his or her charge to the assembly and shares the report by reading it to the entire group.
- The representative hands the report to the clerk of the entire assembly.
- When a report is very long, it is usually read when the group is ready to consider it formally.
- It will then lie on the table until the group is ready to consider it.
- After the reading, the committee representative or another member can move that the report be accepted.
- Usually, the assembly will not vote on accepting a committee report. If anyone objects, however, there must be a formal motion and a vote.
- The fact that the report has been read to the assembly indicates that the assembly has already received it. Thus, there is no need to make a motion to receive the report formally; that has already been accomplished through the reading.

If the committee wants to submit a minority report, it is read to everyone after the majority report is read. The minority report cannot be acted on by the assembly unless a motion is made to substitute it for the majority report. If the motion to substitute is passed, the minority report becomes the report of the committee and is the only one considered.

Adopting the Report

When the entire assembly is ready to consider a committee report formally, someone has to make a motion to *adopt, accept,* or *agree* to the report. Even though these terms have the same definition as far as parliamentary law is concerned, they do carry shades of meaning that can affect their use:

Word	Use
adopt	The report contains opinions and facts but also includes resolutions.
accept	The report contains statements of opinion and facts.
agree	This is used in any instance.

When the motion is accepted, the report becomes subsumed in the entire assembly's work. In effect, it is as though the committee had never existed. However, there is no guarantee that a committee report will always be accepted. Further, there are many other ways that an assembly can deal with a committee report. The following checklist summarizes the possible dispositions of a committee report:

Report Disposition Checklist

The organization can:

✓ File the report without comment.
✓ Return the report to the committee for additional information.
✓ Refer the report to another committee for study.
✓ Give the report to an officer for study.
✓ Give the report to a member for study.

✓ Refer the report to an auditing committee.
✓ Postpone consideration to a more convenient time.
✓ Accept the entire report.
✓ Reject the entire report.
✓ Accept only part of the report.
✓ Reject it and substitute the minority report in its place.

COMMITTEE DISCIPLINE

A committee has no authority to punish its members, but it can report to the assembly as a whole about what has transpired in the committee. The account must be in the form of a written report.

5

Debate

WHAT IS DEBATE?

Debate is the free, orderly exchange of ideas. Debate, then, is the purpose of any meeting. When parliamentary rules are used properly, debate allows members to speak their opinions openly, without fear of condemnation or reprisal. Further, debate gives the assembly the ability to reach an agreement that reflects the will of the majority of members while, at the same time, ensuring the rights of the majority.

OPENING PROCEDURES

Before any subject can be debated, members must follow these three steps:

1. *Address the presiding officer.* A member makes a motion to debate the issue. To make a motion, the member should rise and speak to the chair. The member should address the chair by the preferred form of address. In every instance, the presiding officer must be addressed by the correct official title. If you are not sure how to address the presiding officer, speak with this

person privately before the meeting or see what terms of address other members use. Here are some preferred titles:

- "Ms. Chair"
- "Ms. President"
- "Madame Chairperson"
- "Mr. President"
- "Mr. Chairman"
- "Ms. Moderator" or "Mr. Moderator" (used in religious meetings as a preferred form of address)

2. *Wait for the chair's acknowledgment.* In small meetings, the chair might recognize the member with a simple nod; in large meetings, the chair often says the person's name and affiliation.

Example
The member says, "Madame Chair (or) Mr. Chairman."
The chair says, "Ms. Calabria, business manager of Viceroy Motors."
The member says, "I move that we propose a general stock offering at the next shareholders' meeting."

or

The member says, "Madame Chair [or] Mr. Chairman."
The chair nods at the member to show that the member has the floor.
The member says, "I move that we propose a general stock offering at the next shareholders' meeting."

→ TROUBLESHOOTING

- *Multiple speakers:* If more than one person tries to make a motion at the same time, the one who spoke first after the floor was yielded is recognized by the chair.

- *Chair's error:* **If the chair makes a mistake and recognizes the wrong person, another member can rise to a point of order. One member makes the point of order, and another must second it. This rule does not hold in a mass meeting where the chair is allowed greater latitude in acknowledging people who make motions.**

3. *Get a second to the motion.* Another member must second the motion.

Example
The Chair says, "Is there a second?"
Another member says, "I second the motion."

Note: A call for orders of the day, a question of order, and an objection to the consideration of the question do not require a second.

4. *State the motion.* For the final step, the chair states the motion to the assembly. This step helps prevent any misunderstandings.

Example
"The motion that this organization propose a general stock offering at the next shareholder's meeting has been seconded. It is now open to debate."

If the motion is in writing, it must be handed to the chair and read before it is open to debate.

Until the chair states the motion, the member who offered it can change it or even withdraw it from consideration. After the chair states the motion, the member cannot change it without the assembly's approval. Let's illustrate seconding and/or changing the motion:

1. A member seconds the motion.

    Example
    "I second the motion."

2. The member who made the motion changes it.

    Example
    "Before the chair reads the motion I made, I would like to modify it to say, 'The offering shall commence on October 1.'"

3. The member who made the second withdraws it because she or he no longer agrees with the motion.

    Example
    "I withdraw my second."

    Example
    The Chair says, "Does anyone wish to second the revised motion?"

RULES OF DEBATING

Contrary to what you might have seen in the movies, debate does not involve people yelling or insulting one another. On the contrary, it is a highly structured way to exchange viewpoints and resolve issues.

Following are the commonly accepted rules of debate. They ensure that the debate will be fair and fruitful. Follow these guidelines in the debates that you chair or participate in, unless your organization has passed special debating bylaw provisions.

1. *The right to speak.* According to parliamentary law, every member of an assembly is entitled to speak *once* on a debatable motion unless the assembly has voted to end debate.

- *Speaking a second time:* Every member may speak a second time on the same question unless other members who have not already spoken wish to do so. In that case, the member cannot speak to the same question. Asking a question or making a suggestion is not considered to be speaking to the motion. Such actions are not counted against the time limit.
- *Speaking a third time:* If no one objects, members can speak a third time on the same question. By a two-thirds vote, the assembly can change the rules about how often and how long members can speak during a debate.
- *Speaking more freely:* If greater freedom of discussion is required than allowed for under these rules, the motion can be referred to a committee of the whole (see page 54). Or the matter can be considered informally. Under these rules, members can speak less formally to the motion.

2. *Interrupting speakers.* Generally, a speaker should not be interrupted unless the matter is urgent, for the essence of debate is the free exchange of ideas. The following interruptions are allowed in emergencies:

- Point of order
- Point of information
- Parliamentary inquiry
- Question of privilege
- Appeal the decision of the chair
- Call for orders of the day
- Call a member to order
- Request permission to withdraw a motion
- Request permission to modify a motion
- Call for division of an assembly
- Call for division of a question (a separate vote on divisible parts)

The following motions are in order when a person has been recognized by the chair but has not yet begun to address the assembly:

- Object to consideration of a question
- Move to reconsider (to make the motion but not to have it reconsidered at that time)

3. *Time limit.* In most instances, debate is restricted to *ten minutes* per speaker. This time limit helps ensure that everyone is given a chance to speak and that the meeting is not interminably long. If the membership wishes, however, they may set a special time limit on a specific topic. For example, if extensive debate is anticipated and time is short, the assembly may wish to restrict debate to five minutes per speaker.

- *Speaking on amendments:* A member who has used up her or his time limit debating a motion may also speak on amendments and other motions that may be moved, such as subsidiary, privileged, and incidental motions. A new time limit is allowed because the question is in a different stage of discussion.
- *Transfer of debate rights:* Unless an organization has a special rule to the contrary, debating rights cannot be transferred. In other words, a member cannot yield any unexpired portion of her or his debate time to another member. In the same way, a member cannot reserve any portion of her or his time for a later time. "Use it or lose it" is the rule that governs debate time.
- *Limiting or extending debate:* The motion to limit or extend debate may be used to reduce or increase the number or length of speeches permitted. The motion also may be used to specify how much time shall be allowed for debate on a given question. This motion requires a second, can be amended, requires a two-thirds vote, and can be reconsidered. This

motion is not allowed in committees and generally should not be entertained in boards.

4. *First speaker.* The member who made the motion is entitled to speak first in the debate.

5. *Chair's role.* The chair may not engage in debate unless she or he steps down from the chair. Not allowing the chair to debate helps ensure the chair will remain impartial, protecting the rights of the minority. This rule is often set aside in small boards and committees, where the chair has the same right to debate as other members and does not have to leave the chair.

6. *Appeals.* When a decision of the chair has been appealed, the chair may speak twice on the topic without leaving twice. These speaking opportunities can occur once at the beginning of the debate and once at the end.

When a decision of the chair has been appealed, members may speak once to the appeal. This is different from the chair's privilege; the chair may speak *twice* to the issue.

7. *Maker of the motion.* The member who made the motion may not speak against it. This rule preserves logic: Why would a member make a motion and then work to defeat it?

8. *Seconder of the motion.* The person who seconds the motion is not under the same constraints as the member who made the motion. The seconder may speak for or against the motion.

DEBATE DECORUM

The debate must be confined to the merits of the pending question. Members cannot speak to other issues, no matter how important to the speaker. Despite the clear-cut rules of parliamentary law, debates can become heated and tempers can flare. To help members avoid getting "hot under the collar," the rule is to stick as closely as possible to parliamentary law and to avoid dragging personalities into the debate. Here are some general guidelines for maintaining debate decorum; the issue is discussed more fully in Chapter 10, "Legal Rights."

1. *Referring to other members:* Rather than refer to other members by name, try to say "the member who spoke earlier" or "the member who spoke previously. Officers should always be referred to by title, such as "Secretary Peterson" or "Clerk Sumati." This helps prevent name-calling, assigning blame, and making personal accusations.

2. *Condemning motion, not motive:* Members cannot impugn the motives of other members, but they *can* condemn the nature of the results of the motion—and use strong words! Remember: It is not the member but the motion that is open to attack.

3. *Obeying the chair:* All members should immediately stop talking if the chair asserts privilege. For instance, if the chair rises to state a point of order, give information, or speak on any issue, the speaker must stop talking and sit down until the chair's remarks are concluded. People should not whisper, rustle papers, walk around the room, or in any way disrupt the chair or any speaker. If the chair calls a member out of order, the member must immediately cease talking and sit down. If the member violates decorum or the rules of parliamentary law, the member cannot speak again if anyone objects. The assembly must vote to reassert the member's rights. This question cannot be debated.

ENDING DEBATE

When a debate runs past its course, the chair can use the following expeditious and sensible methods to bring the question to a vote:

1. *Move the previous question (see page 31)*

- When it is clear that the vast majority of members have expressed their opinions and that the assembly is ready to move to a vote, a member can make a motion to move the previous question—that is, bring it to a vote. The chair calls for a vote on the issue. This is called putting the question. Then the chair announces the results of the vote. The motion requires a second, needs a two-thirds vote of the assembly, and can be reconsidered.
- Technically, the debate is not over when the chair puts the question to a vote. It is not complete until the vote has been taken and the results counted and announced. Until that time, any member can be recognized, take the floor, and address the group.
- *Moving the previous question* cannot be used when the motion on the floor is to *amend* (page 32) or to *commit* (page 32). In these cases, the vote applies to the motion to amend or commit as well as to the original motion. If a member moves the previous question on the original motion only, the debate is over and the vote taken. Then a new amendment can be debated.

→ **TROUBLESHOOTING** A motion to move the previous question is not allowed in committees and should not be used in boards, either.

2. *Limit debate (see page 74).* To limit debate means that assembly members can vote to close off the amount of time

devoted to a topic. If this method is used, the motion must be put to a debate immediately. This has the effect of ending debate and forcing a vote.

3. *Close debate.* In the same way that an assembly can move to limit debate, so it can close the debate, ceasing any discussion of the topic. This motion has the same effect as a vote to *limit debate,* described above.

4. *To lay on the table (see page 31).* To lay a motion on the table means to set aside the motion temporarily. Here is how the motion is made:

Example
A member says, "I move to lay the question of [the motion being debated] on the table."

or

A member says, "I move that the matter of [the motion being debated] be laid on the table."

If members want to debate the motion again, they need a majority vote to take it from the table.

5. *An objection to the consideration of a question (see page 35).* This method is used only when a member first makes a motion, before the debate has actually begun. If the objection is carried, it removes the motion from debate for the present session. Here is how the motion is made:

Example
A member says, "I object to the consideration of [the motion proposed]."

SAMPLE DEBATE

Below is an excerpt from a debate that shows how the members debate all sides of the issue freely and fully. The debate concerns whether or not to invite an attorney to be present at the organization's regular board meetings.

Mr. Jefferson: Madame Chair.

The Chair: Mr. Jefferson, board secretary.

Mr. Jefferson: I move that we ask the board attorney to be present at all meetings from now on.

The Chair: Is there a second to the motion?

Ms. Harper: I second the motion.

The Chair: The floor is open to discussion to the motion.

Mr. Jefferson: I have been increasingly concerned about the tone of some of our meetings. There has been an undercurrent of hostility that has caused me distress, and I wanted to ask the membership if they thought that under these circumstances it would be advisable to have an attorney present. I think that the presence of an outside mediator might not be ill advised at this juncture, because it might help us remember the collegiality that we once shared.

Ms. Harper: I am speaking against the motion on two counts. First, I don't think the problems among us are as serious as you say. There *have* been some personality clashes, but when we adhere closely to parliamentary law, we are able to make sure that all members feel that they are being afforded equal opportunity to speak and be represented. I think all we need is parliamentary law; an attorney is a waste of money. I am very concerned about the cost. Our attorney charges us $200 an hour. Since our meetings last two to three hours, we are talking about a great deal of money.

Mr. Malhotra: I am speaking for the motion because I think it is a reasonable idea to have a lawyer present. That way, if we have any questions about policy, we can just ask our lawyer right away. We don't have to wait for the next meeting to get a response.

Ms. Roiphe: I am speaking against the motion because I am concerned that the lawyer might try to take over the meeting. That's always my concern when lawyers are involved. Besides, I don't think it is constitutional to have an attorney present. President Truman told us to get out of the kitchen when it gets too hot.

Ms. Hastings: We know that it is constitutional to have an attorney present because the other firms in this building follow the practice. So I don't think that is the issue here. The issue is whether having an attorney present will smooth over some of the ruffled feathers and personality clashes. I agree with the comments of the member who spoke earlier; I think that if we continue our strict adherence to parliamentary law, we will be able to reassure all members that they will be heard.

The Chair: Is there any further discussion to the motion? (pause) If not, the motion is put to a vote. All those in favor of the motion? All those opposed? The motion has been defeated.

QUESTIONS THAT CANNOT BE DEBATED

According to parliamentary law, not all questions are open to debate. And every assembly has the right to restrict debate on certain motions. According to the rules of parliamentary procedure, the following questions cannot be debated by an assembly:

1. For the orders of the day (see page 41)
2. For questions about the order of business (see page 155)
3. Appeal made while the previous question is pending (see page 35)
4. Objection to the consideration of the question (see page 35)

5. To lay on the table (see page 31)
6. To take from the table (see page 26)
7. The previous question (see page 31)
8. Questions about reading papers (see page 36)
9. Questions about withdrawing motions (see page 36)
10. Questions about suspending the rules (see page 37)
11. Questions about extending the limits of debate (see page 74)
12. Questions about closing debate (see page 78)
13. Questions about granting permission to continue a speech to someone who violates debate decorum (see page 76)
14. To fix the time at which to adjourn (this is a privileged motion) (see page 39)
15. To adjourn (see page 39)

Most assemblies, however, allow members to make brief comments even on undebatable topics, when all members agree. This is true in the U.S. Congress, for example. There, it is common for a small group of members to speak on even the most undebatable questions. Why? This latitude is in keeping with the rules of parliamentary law—ensuring all members free speech.

BREAK-OUT GROUPS

What is a break-out group? In the past, it was common for deliberative assemblies to take one or more short recesses to enable members to gather their thoughts and digest what they had heard in the debate. Increasingly, however, many assemblies are using *break-out groups* to help members give shape to their ideas.

How does a break-out group function? The key to this method is keeping the groups small—no more than eight to ten members per group—and having all members participate. A moderator is appointed to direct the flow of conversation in each group. The assembly is recessed briefly to allow groups to meet. The members of each group discuss among themselves what they have heard during the debate in an attempt to crystallize their thoughts. At the end of the group meeting, the moderators report the group's ideas to the assembly as a whole.

Electronic technology and break-out groups. In the near future, break-out groups will be conducted with the aid of technology. Already we have the capability of using conference calls, computer hookups, and satellite dishes to enable small groups of people from all over the world to conference even if they are not attending the debate. Teleconferencing is becoming an increasingly popular tool in business communications.

6
Voting

VOTING AND ITS IMPORTANCE

Parliamentary law is based on the democratic concept of fair and equitable representation. Unless otherwise stated in the bylaws of the organization or the company, the rule is one person, one vote. Nearly all actions taken by a representative assembly are based on a *majority vote*.

For the purposes of parliamentary law, *majority* means *more than half*.

TYPES OF VOTES

Robert's Rules of Order stipulates three major types of votes: (1) the *majority vote*, (2) the *two-thirds vote*, and (3) the *plurality vote*. The kind of vote taken in each instance depends on the nature of the organization, its constitution and bylaw provisions, and the type of motion being decided. In a few instances, more than one type of vote is allowed. (See the charts in this chapter for further information.)

Basic rule of all voting. No matter what type of vote, follow this basic rule:

When determining the outcome of the vote, be concerned only with the number of votes cast, not the number of people present—since no one is required to vote. The only exception would occur when the organization has adopted a rule to the contrary, in which case it would appear in the organization's bylaws or in any special or standing rules.

Let's take a look at each type of voting procedure, from most common to least common.

1. *Majority vote*

Definition: A majority means more than *half the votes cast*. As a result, *majority* means that more than half the people entitled to vote must approve the motion for it to pass. Majority votes are most often used in elections and for most motions.

When to Use a Majority Vote

- Amend an adopted convention program when specific items have not yet been treated (majority of registered members who are allowed to vote in the convention or two-thirds).
- Adopt an amendment of a pending motion.
- Appeal (a majority vote is needed to overturn the presiding officer's ruling).
- Approve a main motion.
- Adopt bylaws.
- Adopt a constitution.
- Adopt a convention agenda.
- Adopt a convention program.
- Adopt ordinary standing rules.
- Amend parliamentary standing rules in a convention (majority of registered members who are allowed to vote in the convention or two-thirds).
- Amend a pending motion.
- Adopt a report.
- Adopt special rules of order (majority of entire membership or previous notice and a two-thirds vote).

- Amend something previously adopted (majority of the membership with advance notice, majority of entire membership, or two-thirds).
- Approve minutes.
- Call for adjournment.
- Call for an adjournment at a future time.
- Call for orders of the day (can be set aside by a two-thirds vote).
- Commit or refer.
- Confirm.
- Consider a matter informally.
- Consider a motion by paragraph.
- Discharge a committee (majority of the members if they are given prior notice, or majority of the entire membership without prior notice, or two-thirds).
- Dispense with the reading of minutes.
- Divide a question.
- Be excused from duty.
- Fix the time at which to adjourn.
- Fix the time for taking effect.
- Grant permission to continue speaking after being censured for talking out of turn.
- Lay on the table.
- Make nominating motion.
- Propose filling in the blanks.
- Postpone indefinitely.
- Postpone to a certain time.
- Postpone a previously scheduled event (majority vote with notice, or a majority of the entire membership, or a two-thirds vote).
- Raise a question of privilege.
- Ratify.
- Read papers.
- Recess.
- Reconsider.

- Rescind, repeal, or annul (majority with notice, or majority of the entire membership, or two-thirds).
- Refer to committee.
- Reopen nominations.
- Suspend ordinary standing rules.
- Take from the table.
- Vote on a pending motion.
- Withdraw a motion.

How to tally. The following scenario illustrates what we mean by *majority vote:*

Example

Number of Votes Cast	*Number Needed for a Majority*
29 votes	15 votes
30 votes	16 votes
31 votes	16 votes
32 votes	17 votes

When valid: For a majority vote to be valid, the following conditions must be observed:

- The meeting must be correctly called, with members notified properly.
- There must be a quorum present (see page 153).
- Blank ballots do not count in the tally.
- Abstention votes do not count in the tally.

2. *Two-thirds vote*
Definition: While the majority vote is used most often under parliamentary law, other types if voting procedures are also used. One of the most common types of vote is the *two-thirds* vote. This means at least two-thirds of the members entitled to vote must cast ballots on the issue being debated.

When to use: A two-thirds vote is used only in the case of specific motions, normally those that take away certain rights of a person, suspend or change the rules, prevent a question from being brought to the floor, close nominations, close debate, take away membership or office, or give another person additional rights.

When to Use a Two-thirds Vote
- Adopt parliamentary standing rules in a convention.
- Adopt special rules of order (previous notice and a two-thirds vote or majority of entire membership).
- Amend an adopted convention program when specific items have not yet been treated (two-thirds or majority of registered members who are allowed to vote in the convention).
- Amend parliamentary standing rules in a convention (two-thirds or a majority of registered members who are allowed to vote in the convention).
- Amend something previously adopted (two-thirds, or majority of the membership with advance notice, or majority of entire membership).
- Call for orders of the day (can be set aside by a two-thirds vote).
- Call for the previous question.
- Close nominations.
- Deviate from the convention agenda.
- Discharge a committee (two-thirds, or majority of the members if they are given prior notice, or majority of the entire membership without prior notice).
- Extend the time for considering a pending question.
- Limit debate.
- Make a special order when a question is not pending.
- Move the previous question.
- Object to the consideration of a question.
- Postpone a pending question to a certain time or make it a special order.

- Postpone a previously scheduled event (two-thirds, or majority vote with notice, or a majority of the entire membership).
- Reconsider in a committee.
- Rescind, repeal, or annul (two-thirds, or majority with notice, or majority of the entire membership).
- Suspend the rules of order.
- Take up a question out of its proper order.

When valid: For a two-thirds vote to be valid, the following conditions must be observed:

- The meeting must be correctly called, with members notified properly.
- There must be a quorum present (see page 153).
- Blank ballots do not count in the tally.
- Abstention votes do not count in the tally.

How to tally: The following chart shows how a two-thirds vote is tallied:

Example

Number of Votes Cast	Number Needed for a Two-thirds Vote
60 votes	40 votes
61 votes	41 votes
62 votes	42 votes
63 votes	42 votes

Since a two-thirds vote is normally used in situations that affect members very closely, we recommend that the chair use a rising vote (see page 97) to make sure the count is accurate. In very small meetings, a show of hands can be used instead; this method is also favored for its accuracy.

3. *Plurality vote*

Definition: A plurality vote is the largest number of votes given to any candidate where three or more choices are possible. This method is commonly used to elect government officials. The candidate with the greatest number of votes is said to have the *plurality*.

When to use: Election by plurality is possible only when authorized by the organization's bylaws. A plurality that is not a majority of the membership never selects a proposition or elects anyone to office, unless specified through a bylaw provision. Clearly, such a provision is not advised, for it effectively denies the rights of the majority.

How to tally: The following chart shows how a plurality vote is tallied:

Example

Number of Votes Cast	*Number of Votes*
Candidate #1	20
Candidate #2	30
Candidate #3	40
Candidate #4	50

CHANGING VOTING METHODS

Factors to consider. Any assembly can alter the way a vote is taken. When making such a decision, the organization should consider:

• How many members must agree for the vote to be valid.
• To whom the percentage applies. Unless otherwise stated, it is always the number of members present at the meeting.

Recommendations. It is not recommended that an organization base voting requirements on the number of members present at a meeting. In such cases, an abstention would be counted the same as a negative vote; the organization would, in effect, be denying members the right to remain neutral. In addition, members who do not vote because they are indifferent to an issue can have a pronounced negative effect on the outcome of the vote. If an organzation does want to change the basis for deciding a vote from a majority or two-thirds vote to something else, previous notice of the intention must always be given. This means that members must be notified at a prior meeting.

OFFICERS' VOTING RIGHTS

All officers in an organization have the same voting rights as all other members. Except in small boards and committees, however, there are some voting procedures that a presiding officer should consider to maintain impartiality. The following procedures are suggestions, not requirements:

Presiding officers should vote *only* when the:

- Vote is by secret ballot.
- Officer's vote will change the outcome of the election, including instances when the vote will break a tie (passing a motion), create a tie (defeating a motion), or be the deciding ballot in a two-thirds vote.

> **Example**
> The chair says, "There are 22 votes in the affirmative and 22 in the negative. The chair votes in the affirmative, so the affirmative has it and the motion is carried."
>
> *or*
>
> The chair says, "There are 22 votes in the affirmative and 22 in the negative. The chair votes in the negative, so the negative has it and the motion is lost."

→ **TROUBLESHOOTING   An effective presiding officer casts the deciding vote only when so doing would be in the best interests of the organization.**

→ **TROUBLESHOOTING   The chair can never vote twice, once as a member and once as the chair.**

VOTING PROCEDURE

Who selects the voting method? It is the privilege of the presiding officer to select the method by which a vote will be taken. This choice is usually made on the following considerations:

- Size of the group
- Nature of the motion being voted on
- Anticipated closeness of the vote

Although the choice of methods ultimately rests with the chair, any member of a deliberative assembly has the right to suggest the voting method to be used. The member does this by using the *motion on voting,* as the following examples illustrate:

Example
A member says, "I move that the vote on this motion be taken by rising and being counted."

or

A member says, "I move that the vote on this motion be taken by a show of hands."

or

A member says, "I move that the vote of this motion be taken by ballot."

The motion on voting:

• Requires a second
• Is not debatable
• Requires a majority vote

When a motion cannot be debated or modified, the chair should put it to a vote. When a question can be debated, however, the chair should wait until the debate is over before calling for a vote.

Below are accepted voting methods in parliamentary procedure with their advantages and disadvantages.

1. *Unanimous consent.* Also called *general consent,* unanimous consent can be a useful meeting shortcut because it permits the assembly to take action without going through the process of a regular vote. It can be used not only for elections of officers and committee members but even for something as commonplace as approving minutes. Because it is both fair and expeditious, it is an excellent timesaver and should be used whenever there is general agreement among the majority of members as in the following example:

Example
The chair says, "if there are no objections, the minutes stand approved as read."

Unanimous consent does not imply that everyone agrees; it may simply mean that the opposition decides not to press the issue. If one or more members objects, the approval of the minutes (or any other issue) must be put to a vote. A member who objects may not be focusing on the specific issue but on the matter of bringing the issue to a vote that can be counted, such as a show of hands or a ballot.

2. *Abstaining.* An abstention is not considered a vote and is not counted in the final tally.

When to abstain: Members should never vote on any issue in which they have a personal interest.

3. *Changing one's vote.* Members have the right to change their votes up until the time when the result is announced. After that point, a vote can be changed only by a majority vote of the assembly.

VOTING METHODS

In calling for the vote through a voice vote, acclamation, or a show of hands, the presiding officer should always follows these steps:

- Explain the effect of an "aye" and a "no" vote.
- Stand before the group.
- Call first for the affirmative vote.
- Call for the negative vote.
- Announce the results of the vote, and state whether the motion has been passed or defeated.

1. *Absentee voting*

Definition: Votes by members who are not present at the actual meeting.

Advantages: It is a fundamental principle of parliamentary law that the right to vote is limited to the members of an organization who are actually present at the time the vote is taken. Exceptions to this rule must be stated in the organization's by-laws. Possible exceptions include *voting by mail,* which is used in some large organizations that have a widely scattered membership when it is desired to secure a more representative vote than can be obtained in a meeting. If this method is used, it is crucial that the organization's mailing list correspond exactly to its membership rolls.

Disadvantages: The method can be expensive, time-consuming, and difficult to tally.

2. *Acclamation*

Definition: also called *voice* or *viva voce,* this is the method of voting whereby members says "aye" or "no" when asked their vote.

Procedure: There are different forms for putting the question in a voice vote. Sample methods follow:

Examples
The chair says, "As many as are in favor of [the motion], say aye." The chair then says, "As many as are opposed, say no."

or

The chair says, "It has been moved and seconded that [the motion]. Those in favor of the motion say aye. Those opposed say no."

After the vote, the chair announces the results.

Examples
The chair says, "The ayes have it, and the motion is adopted."

or

The chair says, "The nays have it, and the motion is defeated."

Advantages: This is the easiest and most widely used method of voting on an issue.

Disadvantages: Acclamation should not be used when it is anticipated that the vote will be close or when the issue arouses strong emotions and members may wish to keep their votes a secret. In the first instance, rising or a show of hands is preferable; in the second instance, use of a ballot is better.

3. *Ballot*

Definition: Ballots are small slips of paper on which members indicate their vote. If the membership has planned a vote ahead of time, ballots can be prepared before the meeting.

Procedure: Following is the format for such a ballot.

Example
Show your vote with an X.
1. Shall the organization purchase the property at 115A Main Street?
Yes _____
No _____

- The chair should appoint at least two tellers to distribute, collect, and tally the ballots; the number of tellers depends on the size of the meeting and the number of voters. Tellers should be trusted members.
- In tallying votes, incorrectly written names should be counted as long as the intention of the writer is clear.
- In tallying votes, ballots in which the writer's intention is unclear are considered illegal, and are not counted.
- In large meetings, one teller is selected to report the tally. The teller stands, addresses the chair, reads the tally, and hands it to the chair.
- The chair always announces the result.
- A sample tellers' report follows:

Example
Number of votes cast..120
Number necessary for adoption................................61
Votes for motion...100
Votes against 10
Illegal votes 5

> **The chair would say, "The total number of votes cast is 120;**
> **the number necessary for election is 61.**
>
> **"There were 100 votes for the motion, 10 against, and 5 ille-**
> **gal votes. The motion, having received the required number**
> **of votes, is approved."**

One candidate for office: When there is only one candidate
for office and the organization's bylaws require a ballot, the
secretary can be authorized to cast the vote of the assembly for
the candidate(s). If any member objects, however, ballots must
be distributed and a complete vote must be taken.

Voting machines: Very large companies may elect to use voting machines in place of distributing and tallying ballots by
hand. In such instances, be sure that the machines are installed
well ahead of time, that they are fully functional, and that the
operators are well versed in their use. You may wish to demon-
strate the use of the machines to members beforehand.

Advantages: Use this method when it is important or desir-
able to keep members' votes secret. The bylaws may provide
for this method in certain instances. It is used most often in
elections. In counting ballots, two or more filled-out ballots
folded together are recorded as illegal votes.

> **→ TROUBLESHOOTING   Even in very small meet-**
> **ings, do not let members cut up their own pieces of**
> **paper to create ballots. This method makes it very**
> **difficult to keep track of legal and illegal ballots. Al-**
> **ways use an official ballot created by the secretary or**
> **clerk.**

Disadvantages: The method is time-consuming and may not
be necessary, depending on the nature of the issue being decided.

4. *Proxy voting*

Definition: Proxy voting means giving another member the authority to cast your vote through a power of attorney.

Advantages: Proxy voting is used most often in stockholding companies, where membership is transferable, rather than in deliberative assemblies, where it is not.

Disadvantages. Proxy voting is not permitted in ordinary deliberative assemblies unless it is provided for in the organization's bylaws or unless the laws of the state in which the organization is incorporated require it.

5. *Rising*

Definition: Members vote by standing up and being counted. In the simplest rising vote, members are not individually counted.

Procedure: The following illustrates a simple rising vote:

Example
The chair says, "Those in favor of the next regular meeting being held at the Galaxie Conference Center will rise [or stand] . . . Please be seated. Those opposed will now rise [or stand] . . . Please be seated."

When the results of the rising vote are not conclusive, the members can be counted. In small meetings, the chair can count the votes; in large meetings, the chair should appoint tellers to take the count. The doors should be locked to prevent members from entering or leaving. Also, affirmative votes are always counted first. The following example illustrates this voting method:

Example
The chair says, "The question is whether the next regular meeting be held at the Galaxie Conference Center. As many members as are in favor of the motion wll rise and remain

standing until counted . . . Please be seated. Those opposed
will now rise and remain standing until counted . . . Please
be seated."

After the vote, the chair announces the results:

Example
The chair says, "The affirmative has it, and the motion is
adopted."

or

The chair says, "The negative has it, and the motion is defeated."

Advantages: This is one of the best methods for verifying an
inconclusive voice vote and is a fair and effective timesaver in
busy meetings. It is also an effective method to use when a
close vote is anticipated, or in voting on motions requiring a
two-thirds vote.

Disadvantages: Members who prefer to keep their votes on
an issue private may prefer a ballot vote.

6. *Roll call*
Definition: Members respond with "aye" or "no" when their
names are called. Without a specific bylaw provision to the contrary, a roll call vote can be taken only when a motion is made
and approved by majority vote.

Procedure: To take a roll call vote, the chair puts the question to the assembly. The list of members is called in alphabeti-
cal order. The chair's name is called last, and only when it will
affect the outcome of the vote. A member who is undecided
when called can say "pass"; the member's name will be called
again at the end, affording him or her a chance to vote at that
time. The following shows one way for the chair to make a roll
call:

Example
The chair says, "All those in favor of the adoption of the resolution will say 'yes' as their names are called. Those opposed will say 'no.' Those who wish to abstain will say
'present' or 'abstain.' The clerk will call the roll."

Advantages: A roll call vote clearly records how members
voted on issues. This method is especially useful when opinion
on an issue is closely divided and it is important to ensure that
votes are recorded precisely.

Disadvantages: Delicate issues, such as elections, may require a secret ballot rather than the public roll call method. Individuals may be unwilling to declare their affiliations publicly.

7. *Show of hands*
Definition: Members raise their right hands to register their
votes.

Procedure: The following shows how the chair calls for this
type of vote:

Example
The chair says, "You have heard the motion. Those in favor
of its adoption raise their right hands. [Pause for the vote to
be tallied.] Those opposed do the same."

After the vote, the chair announces the results as follows:

Examples
The chair says, "There are 52 in the affirmative and 18 in
the negative. The affirmative has it and the motion is carried."

or

The chair says, "There are 12 in the affirmative and 68 in
the negative. The negative has it and the motion is lost."

Advantages: This method can be used in place of a rising or a voice vote in small assemblies.

Disadvantages. This method does not work well in large assemblies, where it may be difficult for members' votes to be counted. In addition, some members may object to a show of hands and may prefer a secret ballot.

CALLING FOR A REVOTE

Calling for a division. Parliamentary procedure allows for revoting. Whenever a member doubts the result of a voice vote or a vote by a show of hands, the members can call for a division, thereby requiring the vote to be taken again by rising.

Example
A member says, "I call for a division!"

or

A member says, "Division!"

The chair says, "A division is called for. Those in favor of the division will rise." The chair counts the number of members standing and announces the number.

The chair says, "Those opposed will rise." The chair counts the number of members standing and announces the number.

The chair says, "The motion is carried."

or

The chair says, "The motion is lost."

In a very small meeting where all present can clearly see each other, an inconclusive voice vote may be retaken by merely requesting a show of hands. Normally, the presiding officer will take a count on a revote, inviting the person who called for the division to count as well.

→ **TROUBLESHOOTING   A revote is never taken by the same method as the original vote.**

MEMBERS' RIGHTS AND OBLIGATIONS

1. *Right of abstention.* No member can be compelled to vote. As a result, every member has the right to abstain. However, no member should vote on an issue in which the member has a financial stake, as such a vote could cause embarrassment or possible financial impropriety to the organization. For example, if the motion concerns purchasing office furnishings from a firm in which the member has a partial share, the member should abstain from voting on the issue.

2. *Voting rights of members who owe dues.* A member who owes back dues but has not been dropped from membership has the right to vote in all elections and on all motions.

7

Officers and Minutes

NUMBER OF OFFICERS NEEDED
FOR CONDUCTING BUSINESS

The minimum number of officers essential for running a meeting is two: the *presiding officer* (also called the *chair* or the *president*) and the *clerk* (also called the *secretary*). Nearly all organizations, however, add other officers in order to conduct group business more efficiently.

The number of officers and their duties affect the smooth operation of the organization's business. In general, elect only those officers you need to accomplish your work. Establishing too many officers overburdens people and creates a risk that offices will be empty; having too few officers, in contrast, can make it impossible for work to be completed. Make sure the duties of all officers are clearly stated in the bylaws. Review the bylaws often to ensure that they accurately reflect the changing needs of the organization.

Following you will find a descriptive list of officers who can help run a deliberative assembly. The specific officers elected for your organization or company will depend on the following factors:

- Provision of your organization's bylaws
- Size of the organization
- Organization's specific needs

Further, bylaws must specify how the officers are to be elected, their terms of office, and their duties.

RULES OF HOLDING OFFICE

Electing Officers

Most organizations elect their officers from within their ranks; however, unless the organization's bylaws specify to the contrary, officers do not have to be elected from within. The chair of an organization need not even be a member of it! Although this may seem an odd practice, it has the following advantages:

- If an organization is strongly divided and fractious, electing an outside person, neutral person, a skilled leader, may help heal the rifts.
- Large organizations or those with significant assets may wish to elect an outsider as chair to avoid even the appearance of impropriety.

Term of Office

To avoid having officers lose their objectivity or become stale, most bylaws have provisions limiting the term of office as in the following provision:

Example
The bylaws state: "No person shall be eligible to serve more than [. . .] consecutive terms in the same office."

ELECTED OFFICERS

President or Chair

Title. When no special title has been stated in the bylaws, the presiding officer is usually called by any of the following titles:

• President
• Chair
• Chairperson

→ **TROUBLESHOOTING   The chair is the person who runs the meeting even if this person is not the regular presiding officer. For example, if the vice-president is running the meeting in the chair's absence, the vice-president is called "chair" during the meeting.**

Official Company Rank. The presiding officer may hold a different rank within the company—perhaps president, vice-president, executive director, or manager. Conversely, the presiding officer may not hold any other rank within the organization.

Preferred Usage. The title *chair* is the preferred usage today; the traditional title *chairman* has passed from common usage. The title *chair* is a shortened version of the traditional *chairman* but it has another history as well. The place where the presiding officer sits is centrally located, so every member can see this person. This place is called the *chair.* The presiding officer sits in *the chair* to run the meeting. Over the years, the title came to be applied to the office as well as to the seat.

How to Select an Effective Presiding Officer. The presiding officer sets the tone for the meeting and, to a great extent, for the organization as a whole. As a result, it is extremely important to select an effective president. The qualities of an effective chair are listed in the following checklist.

An Effective Chair's Checklist

✓ Helps members follow parliamentary law.

✓ Makes sure that a motion has been made and seconded (if necessary) before allowing debate to begin.

✓ Encourages all members to participate freely in debate and discussion.

✓ Considers only one main motion at a time.

✓ Resolves each motion fully before moving on through the agenda.

✓ Keeps in mind that the person who made the motion is entitled to speak first.

✓ Gives one person the floor at a time.

✓ Restricts debate to the motion on the floor.

✓ Acknowledges that the power of the organization is vested in its members, not in the chair.

✓ Acts in a tactful, fair, and polite manner.

✓ In large meetings, encourages people to identify themselves before they speak.

✓ Is well versed in parliamentary law.

✓ Checks to make sure that everyone knows and understands the question being debated.

✓ Makes sure that personalities remain out of the debate.

✓ Lets people attack the motion, not each other.

✓ Makes sure that members do not abuse motions such as point of order and point of information.

✓ Saves time by using general consent when everyone is in agreement.

✓ Refers complex issues to committees for additional information.

Duties of the Chair. It is important that the presiding officer clearly understand the duties of office. Some of these duties follow.

It is the duty of the chair to:

- Open the session at the specified time.
- Make sure that there is a quorum.
- Announce the business and the order in which it will be considered.
- Recognize members who are entitled to speak.
- State and put motions to a vote.
- Announce the results of all votes.
- Conduct an orderly debate.
- Restrain members within the rules of the assembly.
- Enforce the rules of decorum.
- Avoid wasting time.
- Make the business of the business run as smoothly as possible.
- Inform members about relevant points of order.
- Respond to members' questions about parliamentary rules.
- Authenticate her or his signature.
- Represent the assembly by obeying its rules.
- Declare the meeting adjourned when all business has been concluded.

The chair should bring the following materials to every meeting:

1. Agenda
2. List of all committees and their members
3. Copy of the bylaws
4. Book of parliamentary law

Let's focus on three key areas of effective leadership: knowing parliamentary law, ensuring the rights of all, and maintaining impartiality. Chairs who understand these aspects of leadership will be able to ensure the will of the majority while protecting the rights of the minority.

Knowing Parliamentary Law

• *Expediting business:* Effective chairs use parliamentary law to keep business moving briskly. The more information the chair has about parliamentary law, the more easily the chair will be able to accomplish the order of business and earn the respect of attendees. At the very least, the chair must be completely familiar with basic parliamentary law provisions. If you are the presiding officer, be sure you are familiar with the basics, and bring a copy of the rules with you to every meeting.

• *Hindering business:* Some members will use parliamentary law to slow down the proceedings. Effective chairs, however, can refuse to entertain motions that foster this. If the opposition appeals the chair's decision, the matter can be brought to a vote. Chairs supported by the majority can then refuse to recognize any delaying tactics the opposition makes during the rest of the meeting. Effective chairs know the difference between a faction trying to obstruct business and a group with legitimate concerns.

• *Knowing the agenda:* Be sure to read everything in your packet before every meeting. Underline or highlight important aspects of the agenda, and question the clerk before the meeting about anything you do not understand.

Ensuring the Rights of All

To ensure the rights of the minority as well as those of the majority, the chair must maintain appropriate behavior at all times. Here are some guidelines to help the chair maintain decorum:

1. *Stand to put questions to a vote.* In large, formal meetings, the chair should stand to put questions to the vote and to respond to questions of order.

2. *Use tact.* Successful chairs season their rulings with tact and judgment. In small, friendly meetings, for instance, effective

chairs do not always insist that motions be seconded. Relaxing the rules can help move business along briskly.

3. *Guide members.* Effective chairs help members accomplish the purpose of the meeting. For instance, if a member frames a motion incorrectly, the chair will suggest the proper wording, as in the following example:

Example
A member says, "I move that we lay the question on the table until the next meeting."
The chair says, "Perhaps you mean that we should postpone the question until the next meeting."

Impartial

To maintain their impartiality, effective presiding officers do not participate in any debate or discussion. According to the rules of parliamentary law, the chair cannot interrupt any speaker as long as that person is acting within the boundaries of correct decorum. Unfortunately, some presiding officers violate these guidelines by pushing their viewpoint on the members, interrupting speakers, and generally foisting their opinions on the assembly. Such people should not be chairs.

Chairs who feel that they must participate in a debate can *temporarily step down* from the chair to do so. We do not suggest this practice, however, because when a chair gives up impartiality, the ability to govern is weakened.

Running an Effective Meeting

There are other ways for a chair to make sure a meeting runs smoothly. Here are some suggestions developed by experienced presiding officers.

1. *Advance Preparations.* In addition to reading the agenda and all materials in your packet, make sure the room is set up to

expedite business. For example, if you need a fax, access to conference call lines, or a VCR make sure that all equipment is already installed in the meeting room. Also be sure that all papers you have to distribute have been copied and collated. Experienced chairs often copy separate memos on different-colored paper. Others use little slips of sticky paper, called *flags*, to mark important passages and help them recall key points quickly.

2. *Introductions.* At a first meeting or at a meeting with new members, invite all members to introduce themselves and to offer their affiliation. You may want to use name tags or name plates (if the meeting is small enough to make this financially possible) to help members call one another by name. Be sure that members provide their preferred form of address: Do they want to be called by their first name? By official title? Depending on the nature of the meeting, you may wish to maintain a level of formality and encourage members to use their surnames and a title, or to strive for a level of informality by using first names. Remember: The chair sets the tone for the meeting.

3. *Consideration.* Be aware of every member's needs. For instance, be sure to repeat all questions to help make sure that every member has heard and understood the point. To make sure that voices carry, ask members to stand when they speak. Make sure all memos are typed and clearly reproduced. Be sure your meeting area has handicapped access.

4. *Organization.* Keep track of what is happening at the meeting. You can do this by checking off items on the agenda as they are treated.

5. *Keeping Order.* Do not let any one member or faction monopolize the meeting; be sure everyone has a chance to speak. Avoid digressions. If you think the meeting will be tu-

multuous, you may wish to ask members to submit motions in writing. You may also wish to use a gavel, but this should be a last resort.

6 *Flexibility.* Keep to the agenda, but be sure to accomplish the aims of the meeting. If the meeting is going longer than planned, try to move the agenda. If need be, table items that can wait until the next meeting.

Chairing Difficult Meetings

Some meetings are more difficult to chair than others. It could be that a group of members opposed your election from the beginning, or perhaps a faction is determined to block the proposed company acquisition. Some issues carry great emotional impact, and some members simply may not get along with others. No matter what the cause, use the following guidelines to defuse the situation:

Before the meeting:

- Meet with your board to come up with ways to deal with the situation.
- Consider the situation objectively; don't let yourself become part of the problem.
- Prepare a detailed agenda, including all items that need to be addressed.
- Get the facts! Make sure you have the ammunition to deal with the issues.
- Review parliamentary law and the bylaws of your organization.

During the meeting:

- Follow the rules of parliamentary law closely.
- Eject people who do not belong at the meeting.
- Institute a set of special rules for the meeting, if the membership is in agreement.

- Keep the tone of the meeting impartial.
- Insist that all remarks be addressed to the chair, not to the audience.
- Do not permit members to insult or defame each other.
- If there is extensive disagreement, refer the matter to a committee.
- If tempers flare call a recess to allow people time to cool off.
- Display the agenda to keep people focused on issues, not personalities.
- Maintain your self-control, no matter how great the provocation.
- Use technology to your advantage. If you are using a microphone, for instance, be sure you are familiar with how it works. This will enable you to cut off speakers who become abusive.
- Give everyone else's comments precedence over yours. Be a listener rather than a talker.

After the meeting:

- Go over what happened at the meeting. Learn from the experience.

Using Technology in Meetings

Teleconferencing, videoconferencing, satellite hookups, and conference calls are becoming commonplace meeting tools. Here are some guidelines for the chair's role in these new types of meetings:

- *Know the technology.* As a presiding officer, the chair must be thoroughly familiar with the technology being used. Nothing erodes the ability to govern more quickly than an inability to understand the technology. The presiding officer and the secretary should discuss the technology well before the meeting with a technical advisor, and troubleshoot to make sure everything works properly. If the hookup is especially tricky, the chair can have an advisor standing by to help in case of transmission breakdowns.

• *Remember time changes.* Don't forget that technology enables us to transcend time as well as space. Be sure to schedule meetings at mutually agreeable times, in order to avoid offense and the possibility of disenfranchisement.

Voting and Absence Procedures

Here are two important procedures that a chair must understand: voting and absence.

Voting. Chairs are allowed to vote when the voting is done by ballot and in all cases where the chair's vote would alter the outcome. Suppose, for instance, that a majority vote is needed to approve the purchase of a new telephone system and the vote is tied. If the chair voted with the majority in this case, the motion would pass. If the chair voted with the minority, the motion would be lost. To avoid a conflict of interest, the chair should never vote on a motion that refers to the chair.

Absence: If the chair is absent from a meeting or must leave the meeting for any reason, a temporary chair must be appointed. The procedure depends on the organization's bylaws. In most instances, if the organization has one or more vice president, the most senior vice-president in attendance becomes the acting chair in the president's absence. If there is more than one vice-president, they should be called in order of seniority. If the organization does not have a vice-president, the chair may appoint a temporary chair, called a *chair pro tem.* The appointment is valid only for the duration of the meeting. If the chair has not appointed a chair pro tem, the clerk/secretary becomes the acting chair. If the clerk/secretary is not present, any member can call the meeting to order and see to it that a chair pro tem is elected. The appointment is valid only for the length of the meeting.

Chair Protocol

Do	*Do Not*
Call the meeting to order on time	Start late
Have a written agenda	Arrive without preparation
Treat one item at a time	Skip around
Protect the minority's rights	Speak for members
Preserve the majority's will	Let factions monopolize debate
Use the first person plural	Use the first person singular
Maintain decorum	Allow members to attack others
Keep a quorum	Run a meeting without a quorum
Encourage full participation	Favor a minority
Control yourself	Lose your temper
Take a vote correctly	Lose track of the vote
Use tact	Be overbearing
Be impartial	Try to control others
Quit running things when your term of office is over	Refuse to relinquish power when your term is over

President-elect

Some organizations elect their presiding officer a term or year in advance. This person is called the *president-elect*. The office must be provided for in the organization's bylaws.

Advantages. Advantages to this practice are that it:

- Stipulates who will run the meeting if the presiding officer is absent, incapacitated, or leaves office.
- Allows for a smooth transition into office, because members know a year in advance who will be the chair.

- Gives the president-elect some experience beforehand with the commonplace and unique problems the chair faces.
- Can help expedite business, because the president-elect usually has specific responsibilities, including advising the president.

Vice-president

The vice-president's main function is to run the meeting in the president's absence. Some organizations elect several vice-presidents to deal with the crush of business. In these cases, the vice-presidents take over for the chair in order of precedence: The first vice-president would chair the meeting in the president's absence; the second vice-president would chair the meeting in the first vice-president's absence, and so forth. In most companies, vice-presidents have specific administrative responsibilities as well.

Secretary/Clerk

The clerk or secretary records what happens at the meeting and keeps the organization's records. Many small organizations have only one person to fulfill these responsibilities, larger groups may have two people. The *recording secretary* can also be called the *clerk;* the *corresponding secretary,* the *recorder* or the *scribe.* For the purpose of this discussion, we will use the terms *secretary* and *clerk* interchangeably.

Duties of the Secretary/Clerk
1. Notify members of meetings, called *call the meeting.*
2. Prepare an agenda before every meeting.
3. Take attendance, when required.
4. Keep a record of what happens at the meetings, called the *minutes.*
5. Have the minutes available to all members.

6. Keep a file of all committee reports.
7. Keep the official membership roll.
8. Provide delegates with credentials.
9. Sign copies of all documents required by the bylaws.
10. Maintain the organization's records.
11. Call the meeting to order in the absence of the chair and vice-president.

The clerk brings the following materials to every meeting:

- Minute book
- Agenda
- List of unfinished business
- Membership lists
- List of current standing and special committees, including chairs and members
- Organization's bylaws
- Ballots
- Paper and pen to take notes for the permanent minutes. Increasingly, clerks are using laptop or notebook computers for this purpose.

During the meeting, the clerk:

- Calls the meeting to order in the absence of the president and vice-president.
- Keeps attendance.
- Reads or has printed the minutes of the previous meeting.
- Reads executive committee reports, board recommendations (if any), and correspondence (if any).
- Counts the vote when requested by the chair.
- Records the:
  —Type of meeting—regular or special
  —Name of the association

—Date, time, and place of the meeting
—Name of the presiding officer and those reporting
—Information if minutes of the previous meeting were approved as read, corrected, or mailed
—Business at the meeting
—Treasurer's report
—Correspondence
—Exact wording of all motions, points of order, and appeals, whether they were sustained or lost; the name of the member who made the motions; whether the vote was approved or defeated
—Program topic, type of presentation, names of the presenter(s), and important points covered
—Time of adjournment

After the meeting, the clerk:

• Promptly writes the minutes.
• Sends a rough draft of the minutes to the chair.
• Notifies the chair of any motion that requires speedy action.
• Gives the president a copy of the names of people appointed to special committees, including the chairs.
• Notifies officers and chairs of their election or appointment.
• Prepares a summary of all unfinished business for the president.
• Signs the minutes when they have been finalized.
• Furnishes delegates with credential cards, when necessary.
• Along with the president, signs all official papers, such as resolutions.

Records. As custodian of the organization's records, the clerk should keep a permanent file of the following materials:

• All minutes
• Agendas

- Treasurer's reports
- Constitution, charter, and/or bylaws
- Lists of committees and their members
- Procedures

Computers. Increasingly, all this material is being kept electronically rather than as hard copy. It is extremely important that the secretary keep backup files of all the materials listed here. These can be in the form of backup disks, which should be stored in a safe place. There should also be hard copies of irreplaceable or crucial materials, which should be stored in an alternative site.

Effective Clerk Qualities. What does it take to be an effective clerk? A good clerk:

- Understands the policies and practices of the organization.
- Is prompt.
- Attends all meetings, including executive board and general membership meetings.
- Does accurate and neat work.
- Is enthusiastic and dedicated to the work of the association.

Treasurer

The treasurer handles the organization's financial matters. The treasurer's specific tasks depend on the organization's bylaws. In some cases, the treasurer may just keep track of dues; in larger organizations, however, the treasurer also pays bills, mails checks, and tallies receipts. Nonetheless, in all organizations, the treasurer must submit financial reports that summarize the organization's financial status. In larger organizations, these reports are submitted monthly; in smaller groups, they are prepared only once a year. All organizations that deal with money must submit annual reports that summarize the financial transactions for the year. (See page 159 for a sample treasurer's report.)

Directors

Some organizations elect directors, also called *trustees* or *managers,* who are part of the executive board. The duties of directors vary according to the nature of the organization and must be clearly stated in the bylaws. Some directors, for instance, may be policymakers; others, auditors.

Sergeant-at-arms

The sergeant-at-arms—also called the *warden* or the *warrant officer*—helps keep order in a meeting. The sergeant-at-arms's specific duties, described in the bylaws, vary with the nature of the meeting. In a large annual convention, for instance, the sergeant-at-arms may help set up the main meeting hall, check the audiovisual equipment, and establish security procedures. In an organization that has the power to require attendance, the sergeant-at-arms has the authority to serve warrants, levy monetary fines, and enact other appropriate measures.

Doorkeeper

In addition to one or more sergeants-at-arms, some organizations also elect a doorkeeper, an officer who makes sure that only authorized people are admitted to the meeting. The doorkeeper is allowed to verify a person's identification. The doorkeeper can assist the sergeant-at-arms or work independently, because the two offices are not linked.

Historian

All organizations keep a record of their transactions in the minutes, but some groups want a more personal, anecdotal record of their meetings. Such groups may elect an historian to prepare a chronological, narrative account of events. As part of the group's personal records, these historical accounts are often bound in elaborate volumes and displayed in the meeting place. Such accounts become a valuable part of the organization's papers.

Librarian

The librarian is entrusted with the organization's historical documents. The following materials may be included in an organization's library:

- Letters
- Original manuscripts
- Books
- Illustrations
- Caricatures
- Photographs
- Computer disks

The librarian is responsible for cataloguing, storing, and accessing all this material.

The office of librarian is becoming more significant today. It is increasingly important that the librarian be familiar with computer disk storage. Librarians should also be well versed in the preservation of archival material or should be willing to learn these methods.

Curator

The curator is entrusted with any valuable objects of art owned by the organization, not including library holdings. Included may be:

- Statues
- Trophies
- Sculptures
- Models
- Awards
- Original artwork

APPOINTED OFFICERS

Executive Secretary

Unlike the secretary or clerk, the *executive secretary* is paid by the organization to keep records and, in some instances, to hire, fire, and set salaries. Unless otherwise specified in the bylaws, the executive secretary reports to the board of directors and is responsible for making sure the board's instructions are carried out.

Parliamentarians

Some organizations retain an individual knowledgeable in parliamentary law as an advisor. The parliamentarian receives a salary for guiding the presiding officer, board of directors, and members in understanding and correctly interpreting parliamentary law. Parliamentarians are most often used in large or fractious meetings or in instances when it is crucial that parliamentary law be followed closely. The advantages of using parliamentarians are that they can:

- Assist in answering questions about policy matters
- Help solve small problems before they become larger
- Anticipate problems that may affect a member's rights
- Alert the chair to breaches in conduct
- Help set up meetings and offer useful preplanning suggestions
- Offer classes in parliamentary law to organization members

HONORARY OFFICERS

Honorary officers are individuals—not necessarily members—honored for great distinction or outstanding service to the organization. Although nonmembers are eligible, such awards are most often conferred on members upon their retirement from the organization, with the honorary office matching the office the person held during active service, as the following illustrates:

Examples

Elected Office	*Honorary Office*
Chair	**Honorary chair**
President	**Honorary president**
Clerk	**Honorary clerk**

The title stays with the person for life, unless otherwise specified in the company's bylaws. There are no responsibilities attached to the office. In most instances, honorary officers are given the privilege of attending and speaking at meetings, but they usually are not allowed to make or vote on motions. Honorary officers often sit on the dais at annual meetings, and their names are included on any promotional literature produced by the organization.

MINUTES

Definition. The record of the meeting is called the *minutes.* Minutes are an impartial account of the business accomplished at a specific meeting. They summarize what happened at the meeting in a straightforward narrative style. The minutes do *not* include the following items:

- Personal opinion or commentary
- Direct transcription of meeting dialogue or conversation
- Names of members who seconded a motion, unless specifically required in the bylaws
- Discussion of motions
- Mention of withdrawn motions
- The phrase "Respectfully submitted," which many authorities consider outdated

Preparation. In the past, minutes were handwritten. Today, nearly all large organizations (and many small ones as well) prepare minutes on a computer. This makes it easier for the secretary to make corrections and copies. It also expedites transmission, through such means as E-mail, fax, and modem.

Style. The first paragraph of the minutes contains the following information, not necessarily in this order:

- Date, time, and place of the meeting
- Name of the company
- Type of meeting, such as regular or special
- Names of the officers present at the meeting
- Whether the minutes of the previous meeting were read and approved

Example
At the regular weekly meeting of the Rotary Club held on March 4, 1994, at 6:00 P.M. at Country Farms Restaurant in Farmingdale, the minutes were read by the secretary of the board and approved without correction. Bob Chapman presided, with President-Elect Nancy White and Board Clerk Alana Mello in attendance.

The body of the minutes summarizes what happened at the meeting. There is one subject per paragraph. The body of the minutes contains the following information, not necessarily in this order:

- All main motions
- The disposition of each motion
- Secondary motions
- All points of order and appeals

Example
The chair reported on the installation of the new computer system. She noted that all eight ports are in place and that the system is expected to be on line by June.
On a motion by Ms. Harrison, the board authorized the director to donate $50 to Boy Scout Troop #511 for the purchase of new equipment.
A special committee was appointed to investigate the situation with Apex Roofing, currently in default. The prep work on the roof was completed, but the materials have not been delivered.
The resolution relating to the sale of the Smith Street property, which was tabled last month, was taken up. After amendment and additional debate, the resolution was adopted as follows: "Resolved, That GH International retain Alan Anderson at the sum of $3,000 to appraise the property at 56 Smith Street."

The conclusion of the minutes contains the following information, not necessarily in this order:

- Time the meeting was adjourned
- Clerk's signature

Example
The meeting was adjourned at 2:00 P.M.
                                    Mr. Gotti, Clerk

Here is a sample of completed minutes:

Example
Rafael, Inc.
Board of Trustees Meeting
October 5, 1994
**The regular weekly meeting of Rafael, Inc., was held on
Tuesday, October 5, 1994, at 3:00 P.M. at company head-
quarters. The chair, J. Walcott, presided. The minutes of the
last meeting were read and approved without correction.
The treasurer reported receipt of a bill from Dell Comput-
ers in the sum of $2,000 for a new PC. The question put by
the chair that the bill be paid was adopted.
Ms. Harle, reporting on behalf of the publicity committee,
moved that "the annual convention be held at Galaxie Hotel
in the downtown area." The motion was adopted after debate.
The report of the finance committee was received and
placed on file.
A special committee was appointed to investigate the sharp
rise in graffiti in the main building.
The chair introduced the guest speaker, Professor Christine
Banks, who spoke on educating minority children for the future workplace. At the conclusion of Ms. Banks's talk, the
organization gave her a standing ovation.
The meeting was adjourned at 4:30 P.M.**
                                    Adam Phillip, Clerk

Reading and Approval of Minutes. After the clerk completes the minutes, the document is submitted for approval at the next regular meeting of the organization. The actual approval takes place after the call to order. The chair calls for the minutes to be read, asks for any necessary corrections, accepts the corrections if valid, and asks for a motion to approve the minutes.

Example
The chair says, "Are there any corrections to the minutes?" [pause to allow members to respond]

If there are no corrections, the chair says, "If there are no corrections, the minutes stand as read."

or

If there are corrections, a member says, "I move to amend the minutes by [the specific correction]."

The chair then says, "If there are no further corrections, the minutes are approved as corrected."

→ TROUBLESHOOTING   Remember in most instances the minutes are approved by unanimous consent to save time.

8
Meetings

MEETINGS AND THEIR USES

According to parliamentary law, a *meeting* is

a single official gathering of the members of an organization in
one place to transact business. The meeting must be continuous,
discounting a short break or recess. A meeting may last anywhere from a few minutes to several hours.

With 21st century technology, the *one place* part of the definition can be interpreted broadly. Increasingly, video- and teleconferencing capabilities mean that a handful of people can be
a continent away from each other but still be in the same
"room"! Although they may never even meet, according to parliamentary law they are still holding a meeting.

The traditional image of the definition still lingers. When
most people imagine a meeting, they envision people meeting
face to face, usually in an office, conference room, or hall. The
meeting may involve two directors discussing whether people
in their departments should get a raise, fifty managers present at
a personnel conference in a neighboring city, or a thousand people attending a seminar on hiring and firing. Most likely, you
have attended more meetings that you can recall, and these
meetings have been distinguished as much by their differences

as by their similarities. But one thing all meetings have in common is that they gather people to accomplish business.

A *session* is:

> a series of interconnected meetings devoted to the same order of business. The business is continued from meeting to meeting, often being taken up at the point where it left off.

Parliamentary law distinguishes among different types of meetings and sets up guidelines accordingly. It is important to identify the type of meeting you are attending, planning, or chairing in order to know which rules will help you accomplish your goals.

TYPES OF MEETINGS

Let's investigate the types of meetings you are most likely to encounter and how you can organize and run these official gatherings.

Regular Meetings

* *Definition:* A regular meeting, also called a *stated meeting,* refers to the periodic business meetings of an established organization. The term is used most often to refer to a regular business session.
* *Reason for meeting:* Some organizations meet often for social purposes and may conduct business at these meetings. Other organizations have frequent meetings for business that may have social overtones. Your organization may meet every Tuesday, the first Monday of the month, four times a year. No matter what the schedule, this is considered a *regular* meeting.
* *Time:* The time is determined by the rules of the organization's bylaws.

- *Sessions:* In most instances, each regular meeting constitutes a separate session, as explained earlier in this chapter.

Special (or Called) Meetings

- *Definition:* A special meeting is a separate session of an organization that is held at a different time from the regular meeting. Special meetings are called to deal with urgent matters of business that cannot wait until the next regular meeting. Usually, they can be called only by the chair or the president of the organization.
- *Reason for meeting:* A special meeting is called for the purpose of considering one or more specific items of business. The meeting cannot deviate from its agenda; all business must pertain to the reason that the meeting was called.
- *Time:* Notice of the time, place, and purpose of the meeting must be distributed to members in ample time. Provisions for this should be included in your bylaws. Most organizations allow at least three days' notice for a special meeting.
- *Sessions:* All business at a special meeting is usually considered at one session; it is very rare for business to be carried over to a subsequent day.

Adjourned Meetings

- *Definition:* Don't confuse the name of this meeting with the act of adjourning a meeting. An *adjourned meeting* is one that continues the meeting that came before it.
- *Reason for meeting:* An adjourned meeting is usually called when a regular or a special meeting has not been able to complete all its business within the allotted time. The adjourned meeting takes up the work of the regular or special meeting at the place where it was stopped.
- *Time:* The term *adjourned meeting* means that the meeting is to take place at a certain time and place and the organization

is "adjourned" until that time. Adjourned meetings are often called for later the same day that the regular or special meeting was called, so that the order of business will still be fresh in participants' minds.

Annual Meetings

- *Definitions:* This term is used to define two slightly different types of meetings. The first type applies to an organization that has a general membership meeting once a year. This is the annual meeting of the organization. Perhaps you have attended an annual meeting as a shareholder in a company, as a member of a large organization, or even as an interested party. The term also applies to a group that holds regular business meetings during the year but devotes one meeting a year to reorganizing its board.
- *Reason for meeting:* Annual meetings are reserved for housekeeping tasks that must be accomplished once a year, such as electing officers, reading annual reports, appointing attorneys, selecting official newspapers for publicity, establishing committees, and so on. Strictly speaking, business conducted at an annual meeting can be accomplished at any regular or special meeting.
- *Time:* As its name implies, an annual meeting is held only once a year.

Executive Sessions

- *Definition:* This is a meeting whose proceedings are secret. The term was originally used to refer to those meetings where presidential business was conducted, such as nominating officers or drawing up important treaties. The matter of secrecy is paramount: A member who reveals what was said and done in executive session can be disciplined by the organization. Further, the minutes of what transpired in executive session can be read and approved only in another executive session.

- *Reason for meeting:* Executive sessions are held when sensitive matters are being discussed and information that should not be disclosed to the general membership might be revealed. Such matters normally include anything that might embarrass an individual or the organization, such as discipline, personnel issues, and finance. As a result, those who can participate in executive session are determined according to the organization's bylaws. In many instances, only officers may attend an executive session; in other cases, general members, special guests, and employees whose comments are necessary to resolve a problem may also be included.
- *Time:* An executive session can be held at any time during a meeting but is usually scheduled for the same time on the agenda every meeting. A motion must be made and passed by a majority for an organization to go into executive session.

Boards

Small Boards

In small boards, where no more than about twelve members are present, some of the formality necessary in a large assembly would stand in the way of accomplishing business expeditiously. As a result, the procedures governing such meetings are different from the rules that prevail in larger meetings in the following respects:

- Members are not required to obtain the floor (to rise and be recognized) before they speak and make motions.
- Motions do not have to be seconded.
- There is no limit to the number of times that a member may speak on a question.

- Informal discussion of a subject is allowed if no motion is pending.
- When everyone understands a motion, a vote can be taken without a formal motion being introduced.
- The chair does not have to rise when putting a motion to a vote.
- The chair can speak in any discussion or debate without leaving the chair. This is a very important distinction, for it can change the nature of the debate.
- The chair can make motions and vote on all questions. As with the previous difference, this is a pivotal rule.
- Small boards' minutes are accessible only to board members unless these board members grant permission to organization members to inspect them or unless the organization votes (by a two-thirds majority) to order minutes to be produced and made available to all members.
- Motions to limit or to close debate are not allowed in small committees (see pages 74, 78).
- Motions to limit or to close debate generally should not be entertained in boards.
- In small boards, the rules for reconsideration are as follows: There is no limit on *when* or on the *number* of times a motion to reconsider can be made. Also, reconsideration may be moved by a member who did not vote on the losing side through abstention or absence. A two-thirds vote is needed unless everyone who voted on the prevailing side is present or has been notified of the intention to make the motion to reconsider.

Following are some sample guidelines issued by a multinational firm describing the rules for public participation at annual board meetings. See how many of these guidelines would be suitable for your organization.

Guidelines for Public Participation in Board Meetings

1. Speakers are requested to use the centrally located microphone and lectern, when available.
2. Prior to addressing the board, all speakers should state their name, address, and organizational affiliation, if any.
3. Questions and comments should be addressed to the entire board, not to individual board members, the president, or members of the audience.
4. When a specific topic is under consideration, questions and comments should be confined to the matter under discussion, and not extend to any other matter.
5. A limit of two minutes shall be allotted to each speaker on any given item.
6. A speaker who does not need the entire two minutes may not yield any unused portion of the time to another speaker.
7. On controversial issues, speakers for and against a given topic may be recognized alternately by the chair.
8. Board members may interrupt a speaker for the purposes of clarification and information.
9. Speakers are requested not to repeat points already made by previous speakers.
10. It is expected that speakers will observe the commonly accepted rules of courtesy, decorum, dignity, and good taste. Resorting to personalities will be ruled out of order, as will the use of intemperate, abusive, and defamatory language.
11. Written statements will be received by the board in addition to, or in lieu of, oral presentations.

Occasional Meetings

Parliamentary law and occasional meetings. Not all meetings are held by members of an organized group. For example, a group of people may gather once or twice to achieve a specific order of business, such as donating some equipment or raising money for charity. How does parliamentary law deal with gatherings of a group not affiliated with an organized society?

Electing a chair. When a number of people get together to conduct business, the first order of business is to select someone to run the meeting. It is a good idea to have those people gathered decide among themselves first who should chair the meeting and approach that person informally with the idea. Then anyone in the group can open the meeting by standing in front of those gathered and saying:

Example

A person at the meeting: "The meeting will please come to order. I move that [the name of a person at the gathering] act as chair of the meeting."

A second person at the meeting: "I second the motion."

The first person: "It has been moved and seconded that [name of person to chair the meeting] act as chair of this meeting. Those in favor say aye. [Pause to tally votes.] Those opposed say nay.

If the majority of people present vote for the candidate, the person who made the motion says: "The motion is carried. [Name of the person elected] will chair this meeting."

If the motion fails, the first person will announce this and ask that someone else be nominated for the position of chair.

In less formal meetings, a person may assume the chair by acclamation. Or the person who opens the meeting may call for a chair by asking for nominations, as shown below:

Example

A person at the meeting: "The meeting will now come to order. May I please have a nomination for a chair?"

Electing a secretary. The new chair must then have a secretary elected, following the same procedure, as outlined next:

Example
The chair says, "May I please have a nomination for secretary?"

If only one person is nominated, the chair then says: "Those in favor of [name of the person nominated] acting as secretary of this meeting will say aye. [pause to tally votes] Those opposed will say nay." The chair then announces the results.

If more than one person is nominated, the chair repeats each name and takes a vote on each candidate in turn.

Conventions

Parliamentary rules and procedures are different in a convention setting.

Special Convention Guidelines
1. Most conventions start off with three items:
   - Adoption of credentials committee report
   - Adoption of convention standing rules
   - Adoption of program

2. Delegates should be aware of the feelings of the group they represent so they know how to vote on certain matters.
3. Unless otherwise specified by the bylaws, the quorum is a majority of the delegates who have registered, even though some of the members may have left.
4. There are usually detailed procedures for the submission of resolutions and increasing use of the reference committee to review resolutions.
5. There are usually detailed procedures for nominations and elections.
6. There are usually specific requirements for adoption of amendments to the bylaws.

7. The motion to reconsider an action can be made not only on the day the action was taken, but also on the first business day following the day on which the action was taken.
8. A main motion or resolution may not be postponed to the next meeting because the next meeting is the next annual convention, usually a year away.
9. A tabled motion remains alive throughout the convention. If it is not taken from the table before adjournment however, it dies with adjournment. In this case, it may not be taken from the table at the next convention.
10. All business that is unfinished when the convention adjourns *falls to the ground.* This means that it expires.
11. The only way to carry over business from one convention to the next is by referring it to committee, to the board of directors, and so on, with instructions to this body to report back at next year's convention.
12. A main motion or resolution that is rejected at a convention may not be renewed at the same convention even though the convention takes place over several days.
13. Convention minutes should not be held over for approval at next year's convention. Instead, they should be referred to a special committee or to a board of directors for approval.
14. The motion to adjourn, when made to dissolve (end) a convention, is considered to be an *incidental main motion.* It follows the rules of a main motion rather than the rules of a privileged motion to adjourn.

SETTING UP MEETINGS

What can you do to make sure the meetings you run go smoothly, are collegial, and serve an essential purpose? In today's world, every second counts. Nowhere is this more apparent than in business meetings.

How many meetings have you attended where participants

are at each other's throats and little work gets done? On the other hand, how many meetings have you attended where people treat each other with respect and important tasks are accomplished in a timely manner? It's no illusion that some meetings are more productive than others. Effective meetings share many of the following characteristics:

Successful Meeting Checklist
✓ Meeting participants feel they can trust each other.
✓ Participants are concerned that everyone is represented.
✓ The group clearly understands its meeting goals.
✓ People deal with issues fairly and honestly.
✓ Issues, not personalities, are the focus.
✓ Authority is shared.
✓ There is a sense of collective responsibility.
✓ Participants set high but realistic goals.
✓ People work quickly but carefully.
✓ The meeting focuses on long- and short-range goals.
✓ Members communicate freely with each other.
✓ The group can look at its goals without bias.
✓ Members face problems openly and deal with them before they balloon into major issues.
✓ The needs of individuals are balanced against the needs of the group.
✓ The group uses each person's strengths but does not ignore weaknesses.
✓ The leader guides rather than rules.
✓ Members realize that the way a goal is reached can be as important as the goal itself.
✓ Participants work out individual differences before they affect the entire group.

Here are some surefire steps to follow to make your meetings productive and pleasant.

1. *Do you need the meeting?*

- *Useless meetings:* Decide if the meeting is really necessary. All too often, people seem to meet just for the sake of meeting. Few events are as dispiriting as a useless meeting. People rightly resent having their time wasted. Colleagues involved in a purposeless meeting may also question the motives of the person who called the meeting: Was the meeting called to exercise power rather than to accomplish business? If so, even greater anger may build.

- *Importance of personal contact:* Keep in mind that often there is no substitute for people getting together to debate an issue. Whether in person or through technology, many times nothing can take the place of face-to-face contact.

2. *What is the purpose of the meeting?*

- *Multiple objectives:* Your meeting may have one or more objectives. For example, staff meetings, committee meetings, seminars, and conferences often combine such objectives as to trade information, settle matters of policy and personnel, plan upcoming events, look into new business, exchange ideas, learn new methods of doing business, and settle differences of opinion.

- *Levels of importance:* No matter what the nature of the organization, meeting objectives vary in importance. In most instances, the meeting was called to accomplish one main purpose, with other purposes as incidental. For example, a publishing company might call a yearly meeting to work out next year's departmental budgets. Incidental purposes may include reallocating personnel, rearranging seating, or changing suppliers.

- *Type of business:* Meeting objectives vary with the nature of the organization. A computer software developer, for example, might meet to discuss ways to market new products. A library board, in contrast, often meets to discuss ways to meet patron needs.

- *Watch for hidden agendas:* The stated purpose and the unstated purpose of a meeting are rarely the same. All participants come to meetings with their own goals or hidden agendas. Successful meetings acknowledge and deal with this discrepancy so participants can get on with the stated purpose of the meeting and satisfy everyone's needs.

3. *Organizing and planning the meeting*

- *Plan ahead!* A successful meeting calls for extensive advance planning. Spontaneous, off-the-cuff gatherings rarely use time to their advantage.
- *Factors to consider.* The amount of organization and planning depend on a number of factors including the:
  - Nature of the meeting
  - Size of the meeting—the larger the meeting, more planning required
  - Purpose of the meeting
  - Anticipated mood of the participants—hostile meetings take more planning than cooperative ones
  - Location—it is easier to plan an on-site than an off-site meeting
- *Making a list.* Write down everything you think you will need to have a successful meeting. Don't be afraid that you might miss something; just try to jot down what you think is important.
- *A master meeting plan:* Go back over your list and pick and choose the items you need. Speak with colleagues to see if they can add any items you may have forgotten. There is also another significant advantage to involving people at the planning stage. When people are included in a meeting from its

inception, they have a greater stake in its outcome. This added commitment can greatly contribute to a successful, productive meeting.

• *Keeping good records:* All your planning will be wasted if your records are slipshod. Increasingly, technology enables us to create spreadsheets, tables, and graphs that can greatly aid meeting projections, but none of these tools are of any value if they are lost. Make backup copies of disks. Keep hard copies. Place all materials in a folder and keep it in a safe place. With very large or important meetings, give a copy to a colleague for safekeeping as well.

FINANCING MEETINGS

How much will this meeting cost? Who will pay the bill? Cost is rarely a factor at small meetings, but it can become a prime consideration at major meetings. Imagine that you are in charge of finances for a four-day company meeting at a site outside the company. What steps would you follow?

1. *Speak to the chair.* Start by speaking with the meeting chair or the person to whom you report in the company. Ask if the meeting is expected to make a profit, break even, or even lose money. At sales conventions, for example, a certain amount of money is often allocated for strengthening the company's image. The company may hand out souvenirs, such as pens, mugs, or buttons, and may entertain important clients or potential clients. In addition, special entertainment is provided. There are often local sightseeing trips. Work with the chair or your manager to iron out a budget for the meeting. Make sure the budget is in writing, so there can be no misunderstanding later on.

2. *Speak with the treasurer.* Make sure that you understand the flow of money within the firm. Who will have control over

allocating funds? Approving expenditures? Paying bills? If your organization has bylaws, read them over carefully to make sure you understand the financial structure. You should know clearly what you can and cannot do with regard to finances.

3. *Set up a finance committee.* A four-day off-site meeting requires extensive financial planning. If you have the authority, set up a committee to share the duties. Call a meeting as soon as possible to allocate tasks. Here is a list of some considerations:

- Talk about financial preplanning responsibilities.
- Share information about the duties of other financial committees in similar situations.
- Share the budget for the meeting.
- Explain who has responsibility for the cash flow.
- Discuss the proposed meeting schedule.
- Chart the number of guests, speakers, room, meals, and so on.
- Assign specific tasks.
- Exchange telephone numbers and schedules with other committee members.
- Set up the next meeting.
- Consider setting up all future meetings in advance.

4. *Meet with the chairs of other committees.* Once your committee has met and discussed all the financial issues, it is time to call in the chairs of the other committees and gather their budgets. How much money do they anticipate needing? Incorporate all their financial needs into your budget. Then check the total: Have you been allocated the funds you need to meet everyone's demands? If not, meet with each committee to find places to reduce costs. Hammer out a budget that everyone finds acceptable.

5. *Set up records.* When you have a firm idea of what the meeting will cost, set up a written budget to keep track of the

flow of money. Traditionally, such budgets were created by hand, but today some excellent software exists for this purpose. Such a spreadsheet can make budget keeping a much easier task for everyone involved.

6. *Track expenses.* Planning is only part of the task—keeping track of expenses is the rest. As part of the budget or on a separate document, set up a method for tracking all incoming and outgoing money. Make sure everyone on the committee has read through all the contracts. Check that there are sufficient funds on hand to pay all bills when they are due. Be sure to enter all invoices and payments on the record sheet; after the meeting, you still will have to pay all bills and submit a final report to the conference committee or the person to whom you report in the company.

ARRANGING MEETING SITES

1. *Psychological effect of the setting.* Once you have planned the financial aspects of the meeting, you can decide on a site. Physical location can have a great effect on the outcome of the meeting, for location influences the mood and tone of a gathering. A pleasantly furnished office, for example, helps set people at their ease; a crowded hall with glaring lights and uncomfortable plastic chairs, in contrast, can disorient and upset participants.

On-site meetings: Most small, everyday meetings are held on site, in an office, conference room, or auditorium. Try to find the most comfortable location, suiting the size of the meeting to the room's capacity. It is better to have a little extra space than to cram people into a room.

2. *Off-site meeting locations.* Increasingly, people are becoming aware of the advantages of getting away from the distractions of the office.

- *Video- and teleconferencing:* Meeting off site can be especially important with a video- or teleconference, when it is important that participants not be interupted during the transmission.
- *Hotels:* Traditionally, hotels are most often used for large meetings because they offer all the facilities in one place and are easily reached by different forms of transportation.
- *Conference centers:* While hotels and resorts have long been popular meeting places, a newer trend involves small, centrally located conference centers. A significant number of larger organizations use such conference centers for one- or two-day retreats. Meeting together in an unfamiliar place also affords participants a chance to bond, increasingly important with smaller, more competitive work forces.
- *Advantages of a neutral setting:* When a meeting promises to be difficult, a neutral setting has great advantages. Starting with a level playing field eliminates the home court advantage and goes a long way toward reassuring all participants that the meeting will be conducted according to the rules of parliamentary law, allowing for the will of the majority but protecting the rights of the minority.

   3. *Checklist.* Here are some aspects to consider when you are selecting a meeting location:

Location Checklist
✓ Cost of rooms
✓ Cost of travel to location
✓ Ease of travel to location
✓ Level of service
✓ Site reputation (Is this a location that will attract people and boost registration?)
✓ Comfort
✓ Amenities (tennis courts, swimming pool, golf course, etc.)
✓ Handicapped accessibility

4. *Time factor.* Time is an important factor in selecting a site. If you are arranging a video- or teleconference, for example, be sensitive to the differences in time zones, especially when people around the world are participating. Make sure that you have selected a mutually convenient time for everyone.

SPEAKERS

Often, a meeting is organized around a guest speaker. A law firm, for example, may want several staff attorneys to run a seminar for potential clients; a plastics company may hire a chemist to speak to its production personnel. As always, the larger a meeting, the more planning will go into hiring speakers.

1. *Decide on speakers.* Many times, your organization will know the type of speaker you wish to retain for a meeting. Sometimes you will have a name. More often, you will know you want a person who can speak knowledgeably on a topic. When you have to find a speaker on a specific topic, talk with other people in allied fields to find out who are the most successful speakers and what their fees are. Following are some factors to consider when you select a speaker.

Speaker Checklist
✓ What are the speaker's qualifications for this speech?
✓ What is the speaker's reputation for being well prepared and professional?
✓ Who recommended the speaker?
✓ Will the speaker be available for your meeting?
✓ How will this speaker enhance the program?
✓ Is the speaker acceptable to the majority of the people attending the program?
✓ What is the speaker's fee?

Contact a speakers' bureau: If the meeting budget is tight, consider using a speakers' bureau, an organization that has a list of successful people who will address certain types of meetings for free. Many large newspapers and community organizations have speakers' bureaus. You can obtain skillful speakers through such organizations.

Select speakers carefully. Take your time to pick a speaker who suits your organization's needs as closely as possible. A successful speaker sets the tone for the entire meeting.

Get a back-up speaker. When you are arranging an important meeting, it is a good idea to line up back-up speakers. Emergencies come up, and speakers sometimes do have to cancel. Notice can be short, leaving you in a serious bind.

2. *Generate the right paperwork.* Once you have selected a speaker, some paperwork may be necessary. Your organization may have forms for this purpose; if not, you will have to create your own. Here are some possibilities:

- Contracts (if you are paying speakers a fee)
- Biographical data (for introductions and program notes)
- Supply and equipment requirements, especially audiovisual needs
- Travel forms
- Hotel forms
- Special food requests

3. *Prepare the speaker.* Speakers aren't mind readers. Give your speakers clear written guidelines to make the meeting go as smoothly as possible. Here is some information you may wish to put in a packet for your speakers:

Speaker's Packets
✓ Title and purpose of the meeting
✓ Meeting date

✓ Location of the meeting, including a clear map
✓ Description of the audience size and composition
✓ Fee contract
✓ Official policy on travel reimbursement
✓ Telephone or fax contact numbers (24-hour numbers, especially useful in case of emergency cancellations)

In addition, you should send the following correspondence to any speaker:

✓ *Formal letter of invitation:* Along with the title and the purpose of the meeting, this letter should give ample background on your organization. If your organization has standard brochures, these should be included as part of the description. Make sure the letter clearly describes what the meeting is about and what role the speaker is expected to play. It is a good idea to state the fee and other arrangements here as well.
✓ *Confirmation letter:* After the speaker accepts the position, send a formal letter of confirmation, reconfirming all the important details (date, time, place, topic, duties, and fee). Enclose with it the contract and any other forms the speaker must complete. As a courtesy, enclose a stamped, self-addressed envelope. If the speaker declines the offer, send a formal letter of refusal to help prevent any misunderstandings later on.
✓ *Welcome letter with speaker packet.* About two weeks before the meeting, send the speaker a welcome letter with the packet of information he or she will need.
✓ *Thank-you letter.* After the meeting, send each speaker a letter of acknowledgment. Compliment speakers on their contributions, and thank them for helping to make the meeting a success.

ARRANGING FOR PUBLICITY

The amount of publicity required for a meeting depends on the nature of the meeting and the number of participants. It would be inappropriate to trumpet the regular Friday morning staff meeting; it would be foolish not to publicize a trade show. Companies that run major meetings often establish separate publicity committees, often part of the marketing department. How can you handle publicity for a meeting of your organization?

Small Meetings

Notify participants of a small meeting via telephone, fax, interoffice memo, or E-mail. In some companies, chairs post meeting notices on centrally located bulletin boards or insert the notices in company newsletters. To cut down on misunderstandings, it is always a good idea to follow up a telephone call with a brief written notice. In fact, the bylaws of many organizations specify that members *must* be notified of meetings in writing.

Sending Notices

Following is a sample notice for a board meeting for a co-op owners' organization:

Notice
Members of the Carroll Gardens Owners' Association are hereby notified that the next meeting of the Association will be held in Cleveland, Ohio, at the Meadville Inn, on July 20, 1994, at 7:00 P.M. If you will be unable to attend the meeting, please fill out the enclosed proxy card and return it as soon as possible.

Large Meetings

Publicity for large meetings is a very different matter. Here are some suggestions.

1. *Establish a committee*

- *Seek people with diverse talents.* Balance the members by looking carefully at their different abilities. You will need people who can write crisp, effective press releases, letters, and ads. Try to find people who have worked on past publicity campaigns and are familiar with the options available to organizations of your size and needs.
- *Do research.* If this is the first time your organization has run a meeting of this nature, examine other similar organizations' publicity efforts in these situations. See what approaches would work for your organization.
- *First meeting action:* Talk about the purpose of the large meeting, the anticipated budget, and past publicity methods. Exchange telephone numbers and schedules.

2. *Assign tasks.* Here are some factors to consider as you assign committee tasks:

- What are your printing needs?
- Who will secure printing quotes?
- Do you need mailing lists? If so, who has access to this material?
- How much will mailing cost?
- What electronic means can you use for publicity? E-mail? Teleconferencing? Faxing?
- What outside promotional options are available and appropriate to your needs? Television? Magazines? Trade journals? Radio? Newspapers? Billboards? Posters? Handouts?
- Do you want to hire a public relations firm?
- What are your budget limitations?

AUDIOVISUAL EQUIPMENT

The nature of the equipment needed at a meeting depends on the following factors:

- Purpose of the meeting
- Topic of the meeting
- Number of participants
- Budgetary constraints

A speaker at a local civic association might require only a podium and a microphone, while speakers at a sales presentation might very well request slide projectors, screens, a stereo system, and sophisticated lighting. The facilities and program committees must find out what autovisual equipment the speaker needs. Below is a list of possible audiovisual aids you may wish to consider.

Audiovisual Aids
1. Boards:
   - Chalkboards
   - Easels
   - Pads, markers
   - Electronic boards
2. Slide projectors:
   - Filmstrips
   - 16mm and 8mm sound
   - 35mm slides
3. Sound systems:
   - Microphones
   - Public address systems
   - Tape recorders
   - Music

4. Video equipment:
   • Televisions
   • VHS recorders
5. Lighting/electrical needs:
   • Spotlights
   • Special lights

RUNNING MEETINGS

Establishing an Agenda

What makes a successful meeting? One of the most important factors is planning. We cannot overemphasize the importance of complete and careful planning, especially when a meeting may become tumultuous.

An *agenda* is a plan or program for a meeting. In most instances, the agenda is distributed to members prior to the meeting and is available to guests and visitors at the door. Here are some steps to follow in creating an agenda:

• Have members submit agenda items well in advance.
• Suggest that the clerk ask members for agenda items.
• Prepare the agenda on computer to allow for last-minute changes.
• Distribute the agenda to all members at least five days before the meeting. Consider electronic transmission via E-mail, fax, or modem.

Arranging Items on an Agenda

An agenda can be amended at any time to accommodate the needs of the organization. If a certain piece of business is very important, it can be considered out of order at any time during the meeting. A member must make a motion to suspend the rules, as the following example shows:

Example
A member says, "At this time, I move that we consider [the specific item on the agenda]."

If another member objects, the first person says,

"I move to suspend the rules that interfere with the introduction at this time of the motion to consider [the specific item on the agenda]."

The motion needs a two-thirds vote to carry. The chair, as well as individual members, can move to consider items on the agenda out of order. The next example shows how to make this motion.

Example
The chair says, "The chair will entertain a motion to take up the matter of [the specific item on the agenda]." If no one objects, the chair then says, "If there is no objection, the chair proposes at this time to take up [the specific item on the agenda]."

Following is a sample agenda for a meeting of a medium-sized company.

Example
Meyer, Inc.
Board of Trustees
Regular Meeting
November 3, 1994

   I. Call to order
  II. Reading and approval of the minutes of the September 25 meeting
 III. Reports
    A. Treasurer's report
    B. Officers' report

>   C. Executive committee reports
>   1. Personnel
>   2. Budget and finance
>   3. Publicity and programs
>   4. Building and grounds
>   D. Special committee reports
>   1. Design
>   2. Legal
> IV. Unfinished business
>   A. Roofing project
>   B. Updating PCs
>   C. Classes on word-processing programs
>   D. Terminations
>   E. Appointments
>   V. New business
>   A. Smoke alarm system
>   B. Security
> VI. Adjournment

Creating Your Own Agenda

Decide what items to place on your agenda on the basis of the meeting and its objectives. At an annual meeting, for instance, you would include items on electing officers, establishing committees, and selecting an official newspaper and bank. At a regular meeting, in contrast, you would deal with everyday organization business. Following are some options to consider when you create your own agenda:

Opening ceremonies. Depending on the composition of your organization, you may wish to open the meeting with the Pledge of Allegiance, the organization oath, the national anthem, an invocation, or a special ritual. Plan the ceremony carefully to establish the appropriate tone for the meeting. Some organizations invite guests to participate in these ceremonies; others reserve the honor for members.

Roll call. In some organizations, it is customary to follow the opening ceremony with a roll call of officers. If the organization is very small, there may be a roll call of members as well. To order a roll call, the chair says, "Now, the secretary (or clerk) will call the roll."

Good of the order. The term refers to the general welfare of the group and allows members to talk about the organization's activities, mission, reputation, and so on. Good of the order comes after all new business has been completed. Unlike other motions, which allow members to talk only about the specific issue on the floor, the good of the order allows members to offer comments on a wide variety of issues relating to the organization.

Announcements. This category allows members to share information that may relate to everyone. This item does not prevent the chair from making an urgent announcement at any time during the meeting.

Program. Most often, the program is placed after all other official business is completed. To accommodate a speaker, however, the program may be placed anywhere on the agenda, even before the minutes have been read. Not all organizations have programs; some may have programs on an irregular basis.

Quorum of Members

Definition. A *quorum,* the minimum number of people needed to conduct business at a meeting, is established in the bylaws of the organization. In both houses of Congress, for instance, a quorum is a majority of all members, but this number usually is too unwieldy for a smaller organization. As a result, many small organizations specify that a quorum is the largest number of people who can be relied on to attend.

Why a quorum is important. A quorum helps to ensure that everyone is treated fairly and that a small group does not act without the will of the majority. However, it is usually advisable not to conduct important business unless a majority of members are present, often far more than a quorum. This is one more way to ensure the will of the majority while protecting the rights of the minority.

Possible quorum provisions. The percentage of members who constitute a quorum varies with the organization. Below are guidelines for different groups:

- In organizations that lack a reliable membership roster, a quorum is made up of those who attend.
- In an assembly of delegates, a quorum is a majority of people who have registered, even if they are not currently in attendance.
- In a mass meeting, the quorum in the number of people present.
- In all other groups whose bylaws do not specify a quorum, a quorum is a majority of all members.

Meetings lacking a quorum. Business conducted without a quorum present is not valid. Members can conduct only the following business without a quorum:

- Fix the time at which to adjourn.
- Adjourn.
- Recess.
- Take measures to establish a quorum.

If the quorum is destroyed because members leave the meeting, no other business can be conducted, and the meeting must be adjourned. Members and officers who continue to conduct business do so at their own risk.

Call to Order or Order of Business

Both these terms—which are interchangeable—deal with the order in which business is conducted. Why arrange items in a specific order? It helps members deal with each item in turn, to ensure its full and fair debate. Organizations that meet on a regular schedule, such as once a month, usually follow the same order of business at every meeting. Special meetings, by their very nature, demand that special items be considered in a special order. Most organizations separate the order of business into the following six categories:

1. Reading and approval of the minutes
2. Reports of officers, boards, and standing committees
3. Reports of special committees
4. Special orders
5. Unfinished business
6. New business

The following illustrates this arrangement:

Example: Order of Business

Action	Comment
Call to order: The chair rises.	The chair says, "The meeting will come to order."
Opening ceremony (optional)	Pledge of Allegiance, invocation, and so on
Reading and approval of minutes	The chair says, "The clerk will read the minutes of the previous meeting."
The clerk asks for any corrections to the minutes	The chair says, "Are there any corrections to the minutes?"
The minutes are approved.	
Treasurer's report:	
The treasurer's report does	The chair says, "We will now

not have to be adopted, unless it is a financial audit.

have the treasurer's report." After the report, the chair says, "Are there any questions? [pause] If not, the report will be filed for audit."

Correspondence: The clerk summarizes the correspondence, unless a member requests that a letter be read. The clerk also reads the letters that do not require any action on the board's part, which are treated in the chair's report or under new business. Many organizations include letters in the packet sent ahead of the meeting to members.

The chair says, "Is there any correspondence?"

Committee reports:
Executive board: The clerk gives a brief report of any business.
Action is not required.

The chair says, "We shall now hear the executive board report by the clerk."

Members vote on any recommendations heard at this time.

The chair says, "You have the recommendations of the executive board. What is your pleasure?"

Committee reports:
Standing committees: Before the meeting, the chair speaks to committee chairs to see who would like to make a brief report.

The chair says, "We shall now hear the report of the

_____

committee."

The chair makes a motion to adopt the reports. The motion does not require a second.

The chair then says, "Are there any questions in regard to this report? [pause] If not, the report will be filed as read."

The chair thanks the committee
for all their work.

The chair says,

" _____

committee moves that

_____ .

Is there any discussion to
the motion?"

Committee reports:

Special committees:
Before the meeting, the
chair speaks to committee
chairs to see who would
like to make a brief report.

The chair says, "We shall now
hear the report of the

_____

committee."

Unfinished business: The
chair consults the agenda.

The chair says, "Is there
any unfinished business?"

New business: The chair
and members can bring
new business before
consideration.

The chair says, "New business
is now in order. Is there
any new group for
business?"

Announcements: The chair
announces the date, time,
and place of the next
meeting.

The chair says, "The next
regular meeting will be
held on _____
in the usual place.

Program: If the meeting has
a program, it appears
now on the agenda.

The chair or the program
chair introduces the
program. At the end, the
chair, program chair, or a
member appointed for this
purpose thanks all participants.

Adjournment: A motion is
not needed; the program
can adjourn by general
consent.

The chair says, "If there is
no further business at this
meeting [pause], the meeting
stands adjourned." Some
chairs tap the gavel once,
lightly, at this point.

Minutes

As explained in Chapter 7, "Officers and Minutes," minutes are an impartial account of the business accomplished at a specific meeting. Minutes are recorded by the clerk or secretary and most often approved second in the meeting, directly after the call to order. (See Chapter 7 for a detailed description of the contents of the minutes.)

Reports of Officers

When to make reports. Depending on the bylaws of your organization, officers may be required to make annual reports. In small organizations, officers usually give reports at every regular meeting. In large organization, however, reports are made only at annual meetings. Regardless of the size of the organization or the frequency of the accounting, such reports are made immediately after the reading and approval of the minutes.

Executive reports. In most cases, officers' reports are for information purposes only, although they may carry recommendations. If an officer does make a recommendation in the course of the report, someone other than the officer should make the motion for its implementation. The practice is different in committees, where the presiding officer or other reporting officer can make the motion for implementation.

Treasurer's reports. The treasurer makes a report of the organization's financial standing at every meeting. Unless otherwise stated in the bylaws, the reports are brief and verbal. No action is required on these reports. In addition, the treasurer must give a full written report every year. The report, submitted on the last day of the fiscal year, is always audited. The report should follow these guidelines:

- It must summarize the organization's financial status.
- The information must be presented in such a manner that all members can understand.
- It must follow a standard financial form that fits the needs of the organization.

Example 1: A Financial Statement for a Small Company

Treasurer's Report

The undersigned, treasurer of Jillian Dorans, Inc., hereby submits the annual report for the year 1993–1994:

The balance on hand at the beginning of the fiscal year was $2,000. There was received from all sources $3,456.98; during the same time, expenses amounted to $2,346.91, leaving a balance on hand of $3,110.07. The attached statement of receipts and expenses shows in detail the source of income and various expenses.

Lawrence Fink
Treasurer, Jillian Doran, Inc.

Example 2: A Financial Statement for a Large Organization

Framingham Association
Annual Financial Report
For the period ending August 31, 1994

ASSETS

Current Assets	
General fund	**$ 9,242.92**
Money market	**698,350.73**
Cash in Transit	**200.00**
U.S. treasury bill	**98,049.00**
Petty cash—change	**70.00**
Petty cash—office	**100.00**
Programs	**5,939.63**
Total Assets	**$811,952.28**

LIABILITY & FUND BALANCE

Liabilities	
Accounts payable	$37,485.00
Donations	286.00
Accrued wages	31,907.98
Total Liabilities	$69,678.98

FUND BALANCE

Encumbrances	$21,306.27
General fund balance	755,735.26
Increase—fund balance	(34,768.23)
Total Fund Balance	$742,273.30
Total Liabilities and Fund Balance	$811,952.28

Audits. All organizations have their financial records audited on a regular basis. In most small organizations, the treasurer submits the annual financial report to an internal auditing committee, made up of several members with expertise in accounting methods. Larger firms, in contrast, retain external auditing firms to audit their financial records. All treasurers should insist on regular audits to make sure that any errors are quickly rectified. Once the organization accepts the auditor's report that the financial report is correct, the treasurer is relieved of any errors in computation.

Disclaimer. Until the financial statements have been audited, it is wise to include a disclaimer of liability on the treasurer's report, such as the following sample:

Example
The accompanying interim statement of receipts and disbursements of the Framingham Association as of August 31, 1994, has been compiled by us in accordance with standards established by the American Institute of Certified Public Accountants. A compilation is limited to presenting in the form of financial statements information that is the representa-

tion of management. We have not audited or reviewed the accompanying statements and, accordingly, do not express an opinion or other form of assurance on them.

> **Phillipa Andrews**
> **Treasurer**

Obtaining and Assigning the Floor

Before members can speak in a meeting, they must *obtain the floor*. This means that the member must be acknowledged by the chair and thus given the right to speak. To claim the floor, the member follows these steps:

Example

The person does . . .   *The person says . . .*

1. The member rises and faces the chair — "Madame Chair [or Mr. Chair]."
2. In a small meeting, the chair nods in the member's direction; in a large meeting, the chair addresses the member. — The chair says, "[Name of the person and the person's title or affiliation]."
3. Any members who are not recognized must sit down. They can once again try to obtain the floor when the current speaker has finished.

Debate

Definition. Debate is the process of deciding a pending question advancing arguments on both sides of the issue to reach a consensus. It is a formalized process, structured so as to allow all members a chance to voice their opinions. With the skillful use of parliamentary procedure debate allows people in a deliberative assembly to exchange their ideas freely and come to a decision that everyone finds acceptable.

Rules of debate. How long the debate proceeds depends on the complexity of the motion, how well informed members are about the issues, and the emotional import of the question. But whether the debate lasts five minutes or fifty, every member of the group has the right to participate. Follow these rules to ensure a fair debate:

1. To begin a debate, a member makes a motion.
2. In most instances, the motion must be seconded.
3. The chair must then read the motion to the assembly.
4. The person who made the motion is allowed to speak both first and last to the question.
5. The person who makes the motion must speak in favor of it.
6. The person who seconded the motion can speak for or against it.
7. Every member is allowed to speak on the topic.
8. Remarks must be confined to the motion. Side topics cannot be part of the debate.
9. The time each speaker is allocated varies with the specific bylaw provisions of the organization. Usually, each speaker is allotted ten minutes, but the time can be changed by a motion. Time cannot be transferred, any unused time is lost.
10. Each amendment to the motion creates an entirely new motion. This means that each speaker can once again have the same amount of time to speak on the issue.

11. The chair may not participate in the debate unless she or he steps down from the chair.
12. People must speak on the issue, not on personalities.
13. A motion to move the previous question can be used to end the debate. It needs a second, requires a two-thirds vote, and cannot be reconsidered. This motion is not allowed in committees.
14. When a chair's decision has been appealed, the chair may speak twice, once at the beginning of the debate and again at the end.
15. The following motions can interrupt a debate. They should be used only if the problem is urgent:
    • Parliamentary inquiry
    • Requesting permission to withdraw or modify the motion.
    • Point of order
    • Calling a member to order
    • Point of information
    • Question of privilege
    • Call for division of the assembly
    • Call for division of the question (calling for a separate vote on divisible parts of the motion)
    • Call for orders of the day
    • Appeal the decision of the chair

Questions that cannot be debated. The following issues cannot be debated:

• To adjourn
• To fix the time at which to adjourn
• Orders of the day
• An appeal made while a previous question is pending
• Objection to the consideration of the question
• To lay on the table

- To take from the table
- The previous question
- Questions about reading papers

Handling Motions

(See Chapter 3, "Motions," for information about making motions in a debate.)

9
Setting Up New Organizations

ESSENTIAL ACTION AT INITIAL MEETINGS

Calling the Meeting to Order

Individuals must be notified where and when the first meeting will take place. If possible, contact prospective members by speaking with them in person or by sending a letter, rather than through a public announcement. This will help you limit membership to people who are really interested in the organization. When a sufficient number of invited prospective members have gathered, some member of the assembly steps forward and calls the meeting to order.

Example
Any person at the meeting says, "The meeting will please come to order."

Electing Temporary Officers

The next order of business is to elect temporary officers. It is customary to speak to individuals before the meeting to see if they wish to be nominated for office. Regardless, anyone can be nominated, and anyone can decline a nomination.

Example
Any person at the meeting says, "The first order of business is the election of a chair."

Any person at the meeting says, "I move that [name of person] act as chair of this meeting."

Another person says, "I second the motion."

The first person then puts the question to a vote.

Example
The first person says, "It has been moved and seconded that [name of person] act as chair of this meeting. All those in favor of the motion please say aye. [Pause] All those not in favor please say no."

If the candidate has a majority, the motion is carried. If not, the process is repeated.

Nominees can also be elected by acclamation. The person calling the meeting to order can act as provisional chair and say, "The meeting will now come to order. Will someone please nominate a chair?"

The newly elected presiding officer takes the chair and sets about electing a clerk.

Example
The chair says, "The first order of business is to elect a clerk. Will someone nominate a clerk?"

The chair takes a vote on each nominee in turn until someone is elected. The clerk then takes a seat next to the chair.

Offering a Resolution

The chair then asks a member who was instrumental in organizing the meeting to state its objectives. Other members offer their opinions as well, but no one should be allowed to monopolize the conversation. After everyone interested has offered opinions, the chair should ask a member to offer a resolution. This enables the assembly to take definite action on the issue. The resolution should have been prepared ahead of time.

Example
"Resolved, That it is the sense of this meeting that an organization for [state the purpose of the group], should now be formed."

After the resolution is seconded and read by the chair, it is open for debate. When the motion is approved, it becomes a statement of intent—it does not create the organization.

Drafting Bylaws

One of the most important parts of establishing a new organization is drafting bylaws. As a first step, your organization might begin by soliciting samples of bylaws from other similar organizations. Try to find businesses or organizations that are similar to your own and whose reputation you value. Then your group can compare all the sample bylaws and use them as a template as you draft your own.

To draft bylaws, a member makes a motion to form a committee.

Example
A member says, "I move that a committee of [number] be appointed by the chair to draft bylaws for the society, and that they report at an adjourned meeting of this assembly."

This motion can be amended and is debatable. An organization formally comes into existence when the bylaws are adopted and the membership roll is signed by those who organized the assembly.

Content of Bylaws

The content of the bylaws is determined by the needs of the organization. A list of recommended items follows. Each article is usually designated with a roman numeral.

I. *Article I: Name of the Organization*
   Begin with the full name of the organization.
II. *Article II: Purpose of the Organization*
   The purpose of the organization can usually be stated in one sentence. While the purpose can run longer, it should be as concise as possible.
III. *Article III: Membership*
   Consider including the following items:
   • Classes of members (e.g., active and inactive)
   • Qualifications for membership
   • Fees and dues
   • Attendance requirements
   • Honorary memberships
IV. *Article IV: Officers*
   Consider including the following items:
   • Number of officers
   • How officers will be elected or appointed
   • Officers' duties
V. *Article V: Meetings*
   State when the meetings will be held, including the date of the annual meeting.
VI. *Article VI: Board of Directors*
   To specify the board's composition, the following items should be addressed:

- Who is on the board
- Board's powers
- Rules that govern the board

VII. *Article VII: Committees*

Be sure that this section describes how standing committees are to be formed. In a separate section, explain how special committees are to be created.

VIII. *Article VIII: Parliamentary Authority*

Under this article, state which text on parliamentary law will be the standard reference guide for the organization.

Example

"The rules contained in the latest edition of [name of book] shall govern this organization in all instances when they are applicable and not inconsistent with these bylaws and any other special rules the organization shall adopt."

IX. *Article IX: Amendment of Bylaws*

Be sure to include a provision for the amendment of the bylaws. The following items should be included here:

- Stipulation of prior notice
- Type of notice (oral or written)
- Requirement of a two-thirds vote

Sample Bylaws

A sample model of bylaws follows. See how closely it meets the needs of your organization.

Example

BYLAWS

OF THE _____ ORGANIZATION

Article I: Name

The name of this organization shall be _____

Article II: Object

The purpose of this organization is to _____

Article III: Membership

Section 1: The membership of this organization shall be limited to fifty members.

Section 2: Any adult resident shall be eligible for membership, provided that the resident has been proposed for membership by a current member.

Section 3: The initiation fee is _____. The annual dues are _____, payable no later than January 1 of every year.

Article IV: Officers

Section 1: The officers shall be chair, vice-president, and clerk.

Section 2: The officers shall be elected by ballot to serve for a term of one year.

Section 3: No member shall hold more than one office at a time, and no member shall be eligible to serve more than three (3) consecutive terms in the same office.

Article V: Meetings

Section 1: The regular meeting shall be held on the second Tuesday of every month. In the event of a lack of a quorum, the regular meeting will be postponed until the third Tuesday of the month.

Section 2: The annual meeting shall be held at the same time of the regular meeting for the month of July. The newly elected officers will start their fiscal year at the July meeting.

Section 3: Special meetings may be called by the chair or by the chair at the request of any member for the transaction of only such business as is stated in the call for the meeting.

Section 4: In the case of an emergency, action may be taken by the board of directors by telephone concurrence by a majority of the members. Such action shall be noted in a special memo placed in the minute book and signed by the person obtaining such concurrence and shall be reported in the minutes of the next meeting.

Article VI: The Executive Board
Section 1: The officers of the organization shall make up the executive board.

Section 2: The executive board is the legal entity charged with the management and responsibility for the organization. The board shall establish the objectives of the organization and determine the policy for the development of such objectives.

Article VII: Committees
Section 1: The following committees shall be appointed annually by the chair:
- Finance and budget
- Personnel
- Buildings and grounds
- Public relations

Section 2: The chair is ex-officio member of all committees.

Section 3: All committees are to make reports to the board and act only on the board's recommendations.

Article VIII: Parliamentary Authority
The rules contained in the current edition of *21st Century Robert's Rules of Order* shall govern the organization in all instances when they are applicable and not inconsistent with these bylaws and any other special rules the organization shall adopt.

Article VIII: Amendment of Bylaws
These bylaws may be amended by a majority vote of the executive board after the amendment has been considered at two (2) meetings, providing the amendment was in the call for the meeting.

USEFUL BYLAW PROVISIONS

Now that you have your basic bylaws, here are some useful provisions to include. Remember: You want to establish an organization that will be relevant in the 21st century. Now is the time to think about what your group needs for the future.

1. *Telephone conference call meetings.* You may wish to include a provision in your bylaws that allows your board to meet by conference call rather than getting together in person.

This provision can make it much easier for you to gather a quorum of officers, especially on short notice. As a result, your group will be able to deal with pressing business much more promptly and efficiently.

This bylaw proviso also can save everyone time and make people much more willing to meet their commitments.

How to do it? You can meet by conference call if board members are given sufficient advance notice and at least a majority of the board members participate in the conference call meeting. Install the technology now: If current trends are an accurate forecaster, meeting conference calls will eventually become standard operating procedure.

2. *Conducting business by mail.* You may wish to include a bylaw provision that enables members to conduct business by mail. Use first-class mail, not book rate or fourth class. Have the packet weighed to make sure it has sufficient postage.

In addition to using regular mail, you may wish to consider using a special courier service such as Federal Express, Express Mail, or Airborne Express if the matter is of pressing importance. For a reasonable fee, these organizations and others like them guarantee overnight delivery virtually anywhere in the continental United States. In most instances, the document can arrive the next morning.

How to do it? To be counted, votes must be received from at least a majority of board members within the time limits specified in the announcement in the mail referendum. Action taken by mail should be verified and made part of the minutes of the next regular session of the board of directors. If you are including this provision in your bylaws, the following wording can be used:

Example
The board of directors may submit proposals for consideration and approval by the membership in mail referendums. A __ [insert appropriate percentage] of members voting shall be necessary for approval of the proposals.

3. *Conducting business by electronic mail (E-mail).* This is especially useful when you are really pressed for time and want a verifiable written contact with members. Consider using this method, too, when the matter is too inflammatory or the document too long to justify a telephone call. E-mail also saves the time and bother of going to the post office or copying and packaging documents for courier transmission.

How to do it? If you intend to use E-mail on any regular basis, all members must have access to a computer and know how to operate it. A training session is a worthwhile investment of time and money. Members must be comfortable with the technology so no one can later claim that he or she was disenfranchised.

4. *Conducting business by fax.* Like E-mail, this is a fast, low-cost method for transmitting documents and conducting business, especially with emergency matters. With a brief document, the cost is usually far lower than that of a courier service, for a fax costs the same as a telephone call. Members can use a fax service if they do not own their own fax machine.

Many companies have computers equipped with fax modems. With these devices, individuals can transmit documents over telephone lines without having to print a hard copy.

How to do it? Faxing simply entails slipping a piece of paper into a machine. A training session should take no more than ten minutes.

5. *Bonding.* Officers and agents of the organization responsible for money matters should be bonded. This means that they shall furnish fidelity bonds for the faithful performance of their duties in sums established by the board. In nearly all cases, the organization pays for the cost of the bonds. Consider bonding any member who handles funds in any way, including the receipts or the disbursement of funds.

6. *Annual audit.* It's a sound idea to protect yourself and your organization from charges of fiscal mismanagement. To this end, arrange to have the financial records of the organization audited annually or even more often. In small organizations, you may wish to include a bylaw provision that allows for a small committee of members to audit the books; in a large organization, it is best to hire outside auditors. Regardless of size, any group that handles large sums of money should have its financial records reviewed by qualified independent auditors. All audit reports must be approved by the board. In addition, a copy of the reports should be made available to all members of the organization.

How to do it? Speak with people in organizations similar to yours in size, membership, and purpose. What firm do they use to audit their financial records? Are they happy with these people? Why or why not?

7. *Indemnification.* Officers, directors, employees, and agents of the organization should be indemnified for any costs, expenses, or liabilities necessarily incurred in connection with

the defense of any action, suit, or proceeding in which they are made a party by reason of being or having been a member serving in an elected or appointed capacity. No member or employee shall be indemnified when judged in the action or suit to be liable for negligence or misconduct in the performance of duty.

"How ridiculous," you might say. "We all get along with each other; we don't need anything like this." But we live in a litigious society, and people are slapping each other with lawsuits at an alarming rate. Even a minor squabble could escalate to a major war with alarming speed. Protect yourself and your organization; prepare for the worst.

8. *Election voting.* Here's a simple, time-saving bylaw provision. When there is only one nominee for a given office, consider waiving the requirement for a secret ballot. Members can simply have a show of hands or say "aye" or "nay" when called by the chair. Use this only when the candidate has a reasonable chance of being elected to the office. Otherwise, use the secret ballot to save face and prevent undue hard feelings—and perhaps even reprisals—later on.

9. *Quorum.* You may wish to insert a clause that when a meeting lacks a quorum, then the next meeting of the organization shall be valid even if it does not have a quorum. In some cases this can be illegal, and it opens the doors for various kinds of underhanded dealings. Nonetheless, it may be a useful inclusion for your organization. But be aware that with this provision, factions may develop and be able to manipulate the passage or defeat of specific motions.

10. *Code of ethics.* Consider including a code of ethics as part of your organization's bylaws. This document outlines the appropriate professional behavior for all members and the action that will be taken if members stray from these limits.

Sample code of ethics. Read the following code of ethics

carefully. Then see which articles apply to your organization. Next, get copies of federal and state ethics laws for organizations like yours. Be sure that the final document your organization prepares and adopts does not in any way conflict with government and local laws, which take precedence over any individual laws an organization creates. You may also wish to consult with a lawyer or with a legal team to make very sure that the final document is valid and binding on members. Your code of ethics should be reviewed each year.

Example: Code of Ethics of the _____ Organization
This code of ethics is based on the following articles of New York State law: public officer's law, general municipal law, and the not-for-profit corporation law.
This code shall be distributed to all members of the organization at the annual meeting in January.
As per Article 18, Section 806, of the New York State general municipal law, the following code of ethics shall be in force for the members of the board of trustees for _____ organization.

Article 1: Personal Conduct
Officers of the board of trustees of the _____
organization shall conduct themselves in such a way as not to convey the impression to any person that they can be influenced into giving favors that conflict with their personal duties.

Article 2: Personal Gain
a. Officers of the _____ organization shall not get economic benefit as a result of a contract with the _____ organization. This article is null and void in cases that conflict with the law, including:
• The designation of an official bank or trust company
• The designation of an official newspaper
• Contracts with nonprofit organizations

b. Officers of the _____ organization shall publicly disclose any of the following interests that they may have with a company doing business with, or proposing to do business with, the _____ organization. For the purposes of this code, an interest shall be any of the following:

- Employment with said company
- A financial interest in said company
- A business relationship with said company
- Being related to any of the owners or employees of said company

Public disclosure of any such business dealings shall be made to the officers of the board of trustees at a regular open meeting within the time the officer learns of any of the preceding interests. Included in the public disclosure shall be the name of the company intending to contract business with the _____ organization and the interest in the company that the officer currently has. This disclosure is a matter of public record.

c. Officers in the company then have the right to make an official motion that the disclosure be sent to the organization's legal counsel for advice as to whether the disclosure does indeed present a conflict of interest that is prohibited by law or by this code of ethics. The lawyer's advice shall be entered into the minutes as part of the legal record of the board.

Article 3: Other Censurable Activities

The following activities by officers of the board of trustees of the _____ organization are also censurable under the guidelines of this code of ethics:

a. Investing in any company that will result in a conflict of interest with their duties on the board of trustees

b. Being part of any board transaction in which they have a direct or indirect financial interest

c. Entering into relationships with vendors for pay in matters that are currently being considered by the board of trustees

d. Being part of legal negotiations with any firms that are doing business with the _____ organization without the knowledge and authorization of the board of trustees

e. Using their position on the board of trustees to obtain employment in the _____ organization for their friends or family members

f. Accepting a job that conflicts with their duties as an officer of the board and can prevent them from carrying out their responsibilities to the organization

g. Asking for or accepting any gift under any circumstances in which people might construe that the gift was intended to influence or reward the officer

h. Disclosing confidential information about the workings of the _____ organization

i. Using this information in such a way as to advance their personal interests

Article 4: Removal from Office

In addition to any other penalty prescribed by law, any board officer who shall violate this code knowingly and willingly may be suspended or removed from the board of trustees pending legal resolution of the matter in question. Such an action shall require a majority vote of the board of trustees.

In the event that the officer is found to have violated the code of ethics and New York State municipal law, the officer may be removed from office as per Article 36 of the New York State public officers law.

Article 5: Amendments

This code of ethics shall be amended by a majority vote of the board of trustees after the amendment has been considered at three (3) regular meetings. In addition, the amendment must be stated in the call for the meetings.

Adopted: (date) _____

Revised: (date) _____

11. *Amending the bylaws.* It's important to leave your organization an escape clause, a way to amend the bylaws to keep your group open to change. You may wish to include in the bylaws a provision whereby newly proposed amendments can be submitted at a national convention for consideration.

The amendments should be in writing, and submitted at least 24 hours before being brought to action by the group. To prevent frivolous bylaw revisions, consider requiring a two-thirds vote of the delegate body for the amendment even to be considered.

For a proposed change to become an amendment to the bylaws, it must be approved by at least 90 percent of the delegates present and voting.

12. *Dissolution for nonprofit organizations* This is crucial because the IRS is involved. The assets of a nonprofit organization are permanently dedicated to its tax-exempt status. In the event that the organization is dissolved or liquidated, all of the assets and property remaining after all debts, obligations, and expenses have been paid can be distributed only to organization(s) that are themselves tax-exempt. Such organizations must qualify under Section 501(c) of the United States Internal Revenue Code of 1954 as amended. This shall be determined by the organization's final board of trustees or directors.

10

Legal Rights

LEGAL RIGHTS OF ASSEMBLIES

Any assembly has the inherent right to create and enforce its own laws and to punish members who break the laws. Unless the bylaws state differently, the most extreme punishment possible is expulsion from the organization. In these instances, the organization may publicize the fact that the individual is no longer a member of the organization. This is advisable because it publicly severs all ties with the person.

No matter how tempting the situation, the organization may not exceed these bounds. Legally, you can inform others that the member has been expelled—but you cannot publish the reasons for the expulsion. These must remain private within the organization. Some legal cases have arisen when organizations have broken this rule and the members have sued the organization for libel—and won. Whether the charges were true or not had no bearing on the case, but publishing the charges did.

If you and a majority of the other members of your organization decide to remove an officer or a member, consult an attorney beforehand to help prevent the possibility of an unnecessary and unpleasant legal situation down the road. Here are assembly rights you should know.

Right to Determine Who May Attend Meetings

Members. A deliberative assembly has the right to decide who will be allowed to attend any and all meetings. Nonetheless, every member of a specific organization has the right to attend any meeting unless otherwise specified in the organization's bylaws. For instance, according to the bylaws, members may not be allowed to attend if they owe back dues money or have other financial obligations to the organization.

Nonmembers. People who are not members of the organization, in contrast, can be shut out of any and all meetings, again depending on the organization's bylaws. One way to exclude members if this provision is not in effect is through a motion to go into *executive session,* which effectively excludes all nonmembers from the meeting.

Right to Eject a Person from a Meeting

When an assembly decides that a person is not allowed to attend a meeting, the chair has the right to enforce this mandate. The chair can direct other members to forcibly remove the offender from the meeting.

In a number of cases, the courts have ruled that using unnecessary and excessive force when removing an unruly member opens the organization to prosecution. Since the members are acting as police, they can be charged as police, with using brutality and excessive force.

Many organizations now carry multi-million-dollar insurance liability policies to protect themselves in just these circumstances. These policies cost surprisingly little and are recommended in instances where organizations anticipate or have experienced such problems with members or guests and have been unable to solve them in other ways. Under most policies, the individual officers and the entire organization are insured against such charges.

Right to Investigate a Member's Background

Organizations have the legal right to look into the background of their members. In some instances, members have been called on to testify in these cases. If they have refused, they have been expelled from the organization. In most instances, charges against a person's background are referred to a standing committee for investigation. The committee should be charged to recommend a course of action.

Right to Compel Absent Members to Attend a Meeting

This is called the call of the house and is allowed only in organizations that have this provision in their bylaws. When a quorum is not present, a small number of members can order a call of the house. The call cannot be applied to voluntary societies. A call of the house is made as follows:

- The clerk calls the roll, noting which members are absent.
- Explanations for absent members are requested.
- The door is locked and no one may leave.
- The chair signs a warrant and gives it to the sergeant-at-arms, who "arrests" the absent members at once.
- The sergeant-at-arms then finds the members and brings them to the meeting.
- The chair asks these members why they were absent from the meeting. The members give their excuses, and someone makes a motion that they be allowed to take their seats.
- The members must pay a fine before they can participate in the meeting.

Enforcing these rights through legal means should be a last resort. When it seems that members are going to have to take legal remedies, it is best to exhaust every other possible route to a satisfactory resolution of the problem.

HANDLING DIFFICULT MEETINGS

As a rule, the more difficult a meeting, the more closely the rules of parliamentary procedure should be followed. These rules help all members act with dignity and decorum. They also ensure that all members will be treated fairly and will have a right to express their opinions, which can help defuse a potentially explosive situation. Here are ways to use parliamentary procedure fairly to help run an orderly meeting:

Objecting to the Consideration of a Question

If you feel that a motion is potentially inflammatory and should not be considered by the members of your organization, you may *object to its consideration.* To use this approach, make your objection immediately after the motion is introduced. An objection to the consideration of a question does not require a second, so the chair can put the matter to a vote at once, as in the following:

> **Example**
> **A member says, "I object to the consideration of this question."**
> **The chair says, "Will the assembly consider the question?"**

If the members decide by a two-thirds vote that they do not want to consider the question, it is dismissed at once and cannot be raised again during that meeting.

Defeating The Motion

If the motion is introduced to the assembly nonetheless and does indeed cause the discord you and others had anticipated, the assembly can simply vote to defeat it. But this strategy will work only if a majority of members want the motion defeated. If they do not, the motion will pass, which might lead to even greater disharmony. Trying to defeat the motion through a vote can serve to prolong the unpleasantness, as the debate drags on with increasing rancor.

Moving Motions

In many cases, you will not want to bring the motion to a vote under any circumstances. Perhaps you realize that you do not have the support necessary to defeat the motion. Or you may not want to endure the protracted and bitter debate that such an attempt would entail. In these instances, you may be able to remove the motion from consideration anyway. Some ways to do this include making a motion to table it, making a motion to postpone it, and making a motion to refer it to committee.

To postpone indefinitely. Once a motion has been introduced and discussed by members, you can suppress it by postponing it indefinitely. This is the same as voting it down. This motion takes precedence only over the principal question, yields to any other subsidiary motion (except a motion to amend), any incidental motion, or any privileged motion. It can be applied only to a principal question, not a question of privilege. It cannot be amended.

To lay on the table. This motion is often used to suppress another motion. It is useful when you know you will not be able to pass or defeat the motion being discussed during this meeting and when the debate is getting increasingly out of hand. The effect of laying a motion on the table is to set it, and everything that pertains to it, aside for the entire session. Make sure you have your support in place before you use this method. The motion is made in the following manner:

Example
A member says, "I move the matter of _____ [the topic under discussion] be laid on the table."

A motion to lay on the table has high privileges. It outranks every debatable question and cannot be debated itself. Further, it requires only a majority vote to pass. The motion cannot have any other subsidiary motion applied to it. Clearly, it is an abuse of parliamentary law to use this motion all the time to suppress legitimate debate. But it is a useful way to help control a fractious meeting by postponing potentially explosive discussions.

To refer to committee. Another allowable way to remove a topic that might create serious disorder is to refer the matter to committee. This motion takes precedence over the motion to amend or to postpone indefinitely, but it yields to the motion to lay on the table, to a call for the previous question, and to a motion to postpone to a certain time. In addition, it yields to any incidental question or any privileged question. The motion is open to debate. It is made as follows:

Example
A member says, "I move to refer _____ [the matter under discussion] to a committee."

To decide the composition of the committee, the chair would ask:

Example:
"How many people shall there be on the committee?"

or

"How many members shall the committee have?"

When different committees are proposed, they must be voted on in the following order:

- Committee of the whole
- Standing committee
- Special committee

Point of Order

If some members try to disrupt a meeting by speaking when other members have the floor or by refusing to yield the floor when their speaking time has run out, you may *rise to a point of order*. This motion can be applied to any breach in the rules of the meeting, even when members make frivolous points of order. According to the rules of parliamentary law, you do not have to wait to get the floor to raise a point of order: Members can raise a point of order when someone else has the floor or when a committee member is reading a report. Every member has the right to raise a point of order if she or he notices a breach in the rules of the assembly. The only requirement is that you raise the point of order when the problem occurs—not wait until the matter has passed. Here is how to frame a point of order:

Example
A member says, "I rise to a point of order."

The chair will then ask the member to explain the specific point of order. At this point, the member must describe the matter to which she or he objected:

Example
A member says, "I make a point of order that . . . "

In almost all instances, the chair rules on a point of order. There is no debate or vote. A point of order takes precedence over any pending question and yields to all privileged motions. It does not require a second and cannot be debated or amended. It cannot be reconsidered.

Point of Personal Privilege

If you or other members are being verbally attacked, abused, or insulted, or your motives or integrity are being questiond, you may rise to a *point of personal privilege*. How does a member make a point of personal privilege? Even if someone else has the floor, the member can rise and address the chair.

Example
A member says, "I rise to a question of personal privilege."

or

A member says, "I rise to a question of privilege affecting the assembly."

The member then explains the matter briefly and asks that it be corrected. In most instances, the chair would take immediate action to correct the problem.

Example
The chair says, "The member will state her question."

A member says, "Mr. Chairman, I do not think that we will be able to resolve this matter if Mr. Gatto continues to make personal remarks directed at me."

The chair says, "Mr. Gatto, we must ask you to refrain from attacking Ms. Devane's integrity."

If the matter is so serious that the member thinks the assembly will have to take some action, however, she or he can then make a motion seeking redress. Another member would then second the motion, and members would vote on the issue.

Point of General Privilege

If members disrupt the meeting by talking to one another while someone has the floor, by shouting out, or by walking around the room or otherwise disrupting the meeting, you may rise to a *point of general privilege*. This motion is made in the same manner as the point of personal privilege.

ROLE OF THE CHAIR

The greatest burden for assuring the orderly and expeditious transaction of an organization's business rests with the presiding officer. To be an effective leader, the chair must:

- Have a sense of fair play
- Use good manners
- Maintain decorum even in the most tense situations
- Act quickly to restore order and attention at the first sign of disturbance
- Maintain the parliamentary principles of equal rights to speak
- Protect each speaker's right to protection from interruption
- Adhere to the question on the floor and no other
- Refuse to allow members to resort to personalities, especially when situations get tense and emotional
- Disallow attacks on members or their motives
- Insist that all remarks be addressed to the chair
- Exercise self-control and not be drawn into verbal fights
- Maintain dignity and composure, however great the provocation

GUIDELINES FOR CHAIRS

Here are some ways a chair can help maintain order, even in the most fractious meetings.

1. *Have clear rules.* Potential trouble spots may be eliminated or smoothed out by having a set of clearly defined rules of procedure governing the rights and the conduct of members and guests. Included should be information on who is entitled to attend meetings, to participate in debate, to have items placed on the agenda, and so on.

2. *Beef up security.* If a chair anticipates very serious behavior problems, the chair might wish to post security personnel both inside and outside the meeting room. For this method to be effective, the security people must be highly visible.

3. *Extend courtesy.* The chair can remind members and guests that the best guarantee they have to speak and be listened to is to accord the same courtesy to others.

4. *Grant the floor.* Sometimes a disruptive member can be controlled by inviting the person to speak with the clear understanding that she or he must then allow the next member to speak without interruption.

5. *Call a member to order.* The chair can call the member to order. This is appropriate when the member has committed a slight offense, such as bringing side issues into a debate. In these instances, the chair can simply tap lightly with the gavel and point out the offense.

Example
The chair says, "The member is out of order."

In addition, any member can call another to order, if the situation merits it:

Example
The member says, "Mr. Chair, I call the member to order."

If the chair agrees with the point of order, the chair concurs, states the offense, and then decides what action to take. If the offense is minor, the member can then continue speaking. In cases where the breach of conduct is more serious, however, the chair can decide whether or not the member should be allowed to continue speaking. The chair would then bring the matter to the group and say:

Example
The chair says, "Shall the member be allowed to continue addressing the assembly?"

The assembly would then take a vote. The matter cannot be debated.

6. *Withholding recognition.* The chair can refuse to recognize a member until the meeting has formally come to order and the members have settled down. Most people do not like such treatment and will quickly give their attention to the chair to end it.

7. *Cut off the microphone.* The chair should be familiar with the way a microphone and public address system work. Then, if a microphone is used, the chair can shut it off quickly and with a minimum of fuss if the member becomes abusive.

8. *Take a recess.* Consider taking one or more recesses when the meeting appears to be getting out of hand. Giving everyone a chance to calm down can help temper the situation. It will also

afford the chair an opportunity to consult with fellow officers and colleagues to decide what to do to defuse tension and prevent further problems.

9. *Establish a disciplinary committee.* You may wish to establish a disciplinary committee to deal with these matters. The committee will be more familiar with ways to control members and meetings and likely be more fluent in the bylaws as well. These matters can then be referred to committee for further study and recommendation for action. If the committee is powerful and well respected, the mere threat of the matter being referred to the committee may serve as sufficient deterrent.

10. *Go into executive session.* It can also be helpful to go into *executive session,* which can give officers a chance to confer quietly among themselves. An executive session is any portion of a meeting in which the proceedings are secret. The term originally was used for executive business such as presidential nominations to appointed offices. Today, we use the term for any matters relating to discipline or other matters that should not be shared with the general public.

- The motion to go into executive session is a question of privilege and therefore adopted by a majority vote.
- Any member who violates the secrecy of an executive session can be officially disciplined.
- The minutes of an executive session can be read only in another executive session.

11. *Naming a member.* If none of these methods is sufficient to prevent a member from behaving in an appropriate manner, the chair can "name" a member. This action should not be taken lightly and should be taken as follows:

- The chair directs the clerk to write down what the member has said that is objectionable.
- The chair explains the offense to the member, addressing her or him by name.

Example
The chair says, "Ms. Hollings! The chair has asked you three times to refrain from insulting other members by using offensive personal remarks. Despite these warnings, you have continued in your inappropriate actions."

- If the member ceases the offensive behavior, the matter is over. The member will want to apologize to the assembly or to the individual members who have been offended.
- If the person continues displaying inappropriate behavior, any member can request punishment. Possible penalties include that the member make an apology, be censured, be asked to leave the meeting, be suspended, or even be expelled. The penalty is decided by a vote, which must have a two-thirds majority.
- If the member refuses to abide by the punishment, the chair can take the necessary measures to enforce the punishment. This can include having a sergeant-at-arms or the police escort the member from the meeting.

12. *Amend the agenda.* If a large crowd demands to be heard on a topic that is not on the agenda, nothing prevents members from amending the agenda to include that topic if the officers and members feel that the request is valid and not disruptive. Or the topic can be scheduled for the next regular meeting or for a special meeting.

13. *Adjourn the meeting.* If the meeting has become chaotic and uncontrollable, it is best to move for an adjournment. When

you want to end a meeting, you either have to wait for the speaker to yield the floor or wait until the speaker's time is up. Recall that each speaker is accorded ten minutes under parliamentary law, unless the time has been changed in the bylaws of the organization. As soon as the floor has been yielded, a member can make an immediate motion for adjournment. If there is a second, the chair can put the motion to a vote at once, since no amendment or debate is allowed. If the motion is passed, the chair will say:

Example
The chair says, "The motion is carried. This meeting stands adjourned."

If there is no other meeting, the chair should say:

Example
The chair says, "The motion is carried. This meeting stands adjourned without day (*sine die*)."

GUIDELINES FOR MEMBERS

The chair can't do it all alone. All members are responsible for maintaining an orderly meeting, free from personal attack. Everyone should remember that people generally respond in the manner in which they have been treated.

If a member is repeatedly disruptive at one or more meetings, members can call the member to order and institute disciplinary proceedings. The specific methods of discipline must be included int he organization's bylaws. In the absense of such a bylaw provision, the organization can follow parliamentary authority. What are some possible penalties for disruptive behavior?

- Penalties may include apology, reprimand, eviction from the meeting place, fine, and suspension. All of these penalties should be decided by a majority vote of the membership. Unlike the other penalties, expulsion from the organization requires a two-thirds vote.
- Such drastic action should be used only as a last resort, when all the suggestions outlined previously on these pages have failed to remedy the situation.

DEALING WITH ARBITRARY CHAIRS

Up to this point, we have been describing ways to deal with fractious members and meetings. What can members do when the *chair* is arbitrary and is the cause of the problems within the organization?

First, determine if the chair posssesses these negative characteristics:

1. Refuses to recognize members.
2. Ignores points of order.
3. Ignores appeals.
4. Will not put legitimate motions to a vote.
5. Rejects proper amendments.
6. Interrupts members during debate.
7. Seizes the floor.
8. Violates the bylaws.
9. Refuses to follow the will of the majority.
10. Will not protect the rights of the minority.
11. Is arrogant toward members and guests.
12. Is abusive toward members and guests.
13. Imposes his or her will on the group.
14. Ignores the agenda, deviating from it at will.
15. Adjourns meetings against the will of the members.

If the behavior of the chair of your organization fits five or more of these characteristics, you are dealing with an arbitrary, dictatorial presiding officer. What can you and other officers and members do to deal with this situation? Try some of the following measures:

1. *Begin with discussion.* Start with some friendly, non-threatening discussion. This is best done in private, so as not to embarrass the individual. Have two or three members speak to the chair quietly. The presence of a small group of people indicates that this is not an isolated incident or a grudge on the part of an individual. Having more than one person also helps shield an individual from reprisals, if the chair is vindictive.

2. *Use a point of order.* If the chair continues to abuse his or her authority, rise to a *point of order* at each offense. (See page 187 for information on using a point of order.)

3. *Use an appeal.* If the chair refuses to recognize the point of order, *appeal* the decision and overturn it with a majority vote. It would be wise to make sure that you have sufficient support among the members and officers to overturn the decision before you proceed with this tactic.

4. *Vote no confidence.* If the abuse of power continues unabated or intensifies, a member may vote *no confidence* in the chair. The motion requires a second, is debatable and amendable, and needs a majority vote for approval. This motion is not as strong a condemnation as a vote of *censure* (see below).

5. *Censure.* If these methods do not work, and the chair's behavior continues to interfere with the orderly conduct of business, a motion can be made to *censure* the chair. Censure is an expression of indignation, a reprimand aimed at preventing further offending actions. This is a very serious charge against a chair (or against any other officer, for that matter) and should be brought only after extensive reflection. To censure a chair, the following steps must be taken, in this order:

1. *Make the motion.* A member makes a motion for censure.
2. *Vote on the motion.* Since the motion logically cannot be put to a vote by the president, it is put to a vote by the vice-president. If the vice-president is not willing, the task falls to the clerk. If neither is present or willing to entertain the motion, it is put to a vote by the maker of the motion.
3. *Debate the motion.* The chair is free to participate in the debate of the motion. This is in sharp contrast to the usual procedure, whereby a chair cannot participate in the debate.

This motion needs a second, can be debated and amended, and requires a majority to pass.

6. *Remove from office.* In extreme cases, if the problem becomes unbearable, steps may be taken to remove the individual from office. This is the strongest action that can be brought against an officer, and it is best not to resort to this extreme measure unless the situation truly calls for it and the organization cannot wait until the next regularly scheduled election to vote the person out of office. If the members do decide to take this action, it must be done by following the bylaws of the organization to the letter. Here are the steps to follow:

1. *Rescind the election.* If the bylaws read, "The chair may serve for ——— year(s) *or* until his/her successor is elected," the election of the chair can be rescinded by a two-thirds vote and a successor elected for the remainder of the term.
2. *Amend the bylaws.* If the bylaws are specific as to the length of the term of office or if they state that the chair shall serve for ——— years *and* until a successor is elected, then the president can be deposed only by amending the bylaws to shorten the term of office or by holding a formal trial after charges have been brought.
3. *Hold a formal trial.* This is the strongest and potentially

most disruptive way of unseating a chair. There are very specific steps to follow:

- *Give notice.* The members must instruct the clerk to appear before the members at a meeting, where the member can hear and respond to the charges. The clerk is charged with informing the member of the meeting and giving him or her a copy of the charges. At this time, the member should be given a chance to show cause why he or she should not be expelled from the organization.

- *Investigate the matter.* A committee of members whose character is above reproach should be formed to look into the matter. Use the following format for the resolution to form the committee and describe its duties:

Example
Resolved, That a committee of [number of people] be formed to investigate the [specific charges] levied against [name of member] and be instructed to report its findings and resolutions.

The committee does not have any power to compel anyone to give testimony, especially the accused. Nonetheless, a sense of fair play demands that the committee meet with the accused to get her or his side of the story.

- *"Arrest."* After a member has formally been charged, the member is considered to be "under arrest." Until the case is resolved, he or she does not have any rights in the organization. In some cases, this requirement is waived, depending on the nature of the accusation and the feelings of the members.
- *Report on the matter.* If the committee finds that the member is not guilty of any breach of conduct, they should report to that effect and the matter is dropped. But if the committee finds that there is a basis for the accusation, they should prepare a written report and have every member of the committee

sign it. A possible format for the report follows. The *charge* explains the offense, the *specifications* give specific examples of what the accused is said to have done. For example, the charge might be conduct unbecoming a member of the society; the specifications might be stealing money from the organization's treasury or physically assaulting another member.

Example
Resolved, That [member's name] is cited to appear on March 25, 1994, at 9:00 A.M. for a trial to show cause why [he or she] should not be expelled from the [name of the organization] on the following charge:
Charge: Conduct unbecoming to a member of this organization.
Specification 1: [specific complaint against the member]
Specification 2: [specific complaint against the member]
Resolved: That a trial consisting of [names of committee members] will hear the case.

• *Hold the trial.* In most instances, the trial is held at a later date, not at the same meeting where the member was charged. Usually, the member is given at least 30 days to respond to the charges and to prepare for the trial. The member must be given official notice that he or she is going to be tried. The notice should be sent out by the clerk using the following format:

Example
Dear [name of the accused member]:
The [name of organization] adopted the following resolution at its April 25th meeting: [text of resolution]
You are hereby cited to appear for a trial at the time indicated above to show cause why you should not be expelled from this organization.
    Sincerely,
    [name of clerk]

- *Present evidence.* Evidence is presented at the trial. In most instances, the report of the disciplinary committee is sufficient. The chair of the committee will read the report and give any additional information required. The accused person should then be allowed to present his or her side of the case and call witnesses, if desired. As in a conventional trial, both sides are allowed to examine all witnesses and present rebuttals. If the accused does not attend, the trial is held anyway.
- *Present a defense.* The accused person has the right to be represented by an attorney, but the attorney would have to be a member of the organization. If the attorney breaches the bounds of acceptable behavior, he or she is also open for censure, according to the bylaws of the organization. The order of events at a trial are as follows:

1. The chair asks the clerk to read the charges.
2. The chair asks the accused whether he or she pleads *guilty* or *not guilty* to each of the specifications and then to the charge.
3. If the accused pleads *guilty,* the trial is not held. Instead, the penalty is decided.
4. If the accused pleads *not guilty,* the trial is held in this order:
   - Both sides present opening statements.
   - Witnesses testify.
   - Rebuttal witnesses testify.
   - Both sides present closing arguments.
   - *Deliberate.* When all the evidence has been produced, the members should deliberate the issue without the accused person present.
   - *Vote.* When the deliberations are completed, the group should take a vote on the issue. No one should be expelled without at least a two-thirds vote in favor of the action. A quorum must be present for the voting. After

the vote, the accused is called back and informed of the decision.

Fortunately, parliamentary law provides many different ways to maintain order and decorum. These methods usually enable members to avoid the disruption of official censure and trial. One of the most effective ways to keep an organization running smoothly is to create bylaws that clearly state the mission of the organization and the equitable way that everyone will be treated. When all members feel they are being treated fairly, there is much less chance of disruption.

11

Glossary

This glossary includes the most commonly used terms in parliamentary procedure. Read through the terms a few times to familiarize yourself with the language of parliamentary law. Then use the glossary as a guide when you participate in—or run—meetings.

Abstain
Decide not to vote on an issue. To abstain, the member answers "present" or "abstain" in a roll call vote.

Accept a report
Adopt a report, not just receive it.

Adjourn
End a meeting officially. Adjournment is accomplished either by direct vote or by unanimous consent. It is not a debatable motion.

Adjourn *sine die*
Adjourn "without day." The term usually refers to the close of a session of several meetings.

Agenda
List of items of business that the people attending a meeting consider. An agenda has a specific arrangement and content.

Amend
Change a resolution or a motion by adding, striking out, or substituting a word or phrase.

Amend the amendment
This motion must pertain to the amendment to which it is attached and must be disposed of before another amendment can be added. No more than two amendments can be considered by the assembly at the same time.

Appeal   A question that occurs when a member of the assembly or a delegate to a convention questions (appeals) a decision by the chair because the person believes that an error in parliamentary procedure has occurred. An appeal must have a second. The decision of the chair is sustained by a majority vote or a tie vote.

Asssembly   Organized group of people meeting to conduct business.

Ballot   A written vote that assures the secrecy of the individual's election decision.

Board   Administrative, managerial, or quasi-judicial body of officials who are elected or appointed and given specific authority to set policy for an organization. A board, unlike a committee, is considered to be a form of assembly.

Bylaws   Set of rules by which an organization conducts business. The bylaws may not be suspended, but they can be amended.

Call for orders of the day   Motion bringing to the chair's attention the fact that specific item of business was due to come up in the meeting at a specific time.

Chair   Presiding officer of an organization, usually the same as the president. The chair may also be called *president* or *presiding officer,* depending on the will of the majority of people in an organization.

Committee   Group of members elected or appointed by an organization to consider or take action on a specific subject. Unlike a board, a committee is not considered to be a form of assembly.

Committee of the whole   Device that enables the entire assembly to operate under committee rules, which are less stringent.

Congress   U.S. House of Representatives (not the Senate).

Consent   Also called *unanimous consent* or *general consent,* this provision allows for consent without a formal vote.

Convention rules	Rules determined by the delegates to the convention to provide an orderly procedure to accomplish business most efficiently within a convention period. A two-thirds vote is needed to adopt convention rules or to effect any change in the rules after they have been adopted.
Debate	Discuss the merits of a specific question.
Decorum	Proper way of acting in a debate, including refraining from attacking someone's motives, addressing all remarks through the chair, avoiding use of members' names, refraining from speaking against your own motion, and refraining from disturbing the assembly.
Divide a motion	Motion asking that a long or complex main motion, such as a series of resolutions, be considered in individual sections rather than as a whole motion. This can help members understand the issues under discussion and so make much more informed decisions and rulings.
Division	Demand that delegates retake a vote. Division can be ordered by the chair of a meeting or by individual delegates.
Division of the question	Separation of the parts of a motion to be considered and voted on as if they were separate motions.
Ex officio	Membership on a board or a committee by virtue of holding an office in the organization. Depending on the organization's bylaws, the ex officio member may have all the rights of a regular member (such as making motions and voting) but none of the obligations.
Extend debate	Officially extend the amount of time that members have to debate an issue.
Floor	Right of a person to address a meeting and have the members' undivided attention.
Gavel	Small hammer representing the authority of

	the presiding officer. Many chairs open and close a meeting by rapping once or twice with the gavel.
Incidental motions	Motions relating to the pending business or to the business on the floor.
Lay on the table	See Table.
Limit debate	Officially restrict the amount of time that members may talk about an issue.
Main motion	Method of introducing new business to an assembly. Only one main motion can be under consideration at a time.
Majority	More than half of the members present and voting on an issue. Those who do not vote are not counted in the final tally.
Meeting	Members assembled to transact business.
Minutes	Record of the proceedings of a deliberative assembly.
Motions	Proposal for action by the group. A motion is introduced with the words, "I move that _____," with the specific motion filling in the blank.
Motion on voting	Motion proposing that a vote be taken in a specific way.
New business	Items that do not belong under any other class of business but are being introduced to the membership for the first time.
Objection	Occurs when a member is strongly opposed to the main motion. A member can then rise and call out, "Mr. (or Ms.) Chair, I object to the consideration of that question," immediately after it has been stated by the chair. Do not confuse this action with the phrase "I object." The only time the phrase "I object" should be used is when the chair attempts to pass a motion by unanimous consent and someone objects to doing so.
Order of business	Order in which the items on the agenda are discussed at the meeting. The order of busi-

ness helps ensure that all items are dealt with in a fair and timely manner.

Order of the day
Privileged motion by which a member can demand that the meeting follow its agenda.

Parliamentary inquiry
Request for an immediate answer to a question concerning parliamentary law. It is directed at the chair, who may turn to the parliamentarian (if the organization has a person in that role) for assistance.

Pending business
Business that is on the floor.

Plurality
Number of votes given to the candidate with the most votes where there are three or more choices. A plurality does not have to constitute a majority of votes for any one candidate.

Point of information
Request directed to the chair for an immediate answer to a question concerning the background or content of a motion or a resolution. The information requested does not pertain to parliamentary procedure, for that is covered under "parliamentary inquiry."

Point of order
Point raised against any proceeding or motion that the member believes is a violation of the rules. It must be raised at the time of the alleged infraction. The chair rules on the validity of the point of order. This ruling can be appealed.

Point of personal privilege
Request for the immediate consideration of a matter affecting the comfort, safety, or orderliness of a member.

Postpone indefinitely
Reject the main motion in a decorous manner. If this motion is passed, the main motion cannot be brought up again in its original form at that particular session.

Postpone to a definite time
Defer consideration of a main motion and all attached motions until a future date. At that time, the matter will be brought up again under unfinished business. To make sure the motion gets priority consideration, it should

be made a special order, in which case the motion to postpone requires a two-thirds vote.

Precedence of motion Claim of a motion to the "right of way" over another motion.

Previous question Motion to close debate and vote immediately on a motion. Moving the previous question requires a second, is not debatable, and needs a two-thirds vote for adoption.

Previous question in its entirety Motion to close debate on a main motion (a resolution and all pending questions). It needs a two-thirds vote for adoption.

Privileged motion Motion that has to do with pressing matter of of importance. A privileged motion can interrupt any business on the floor. The five privileged motions fit into an order of precedence.

Program Agenda for a specific meeting, including time for speakers, meals, and other social matters.

Pro tem Temporary.

Quorum Number of members needed to conduct business. A quorum is established by the bylaws of an organization.

Rank of motion See Precedence of motion.

Recess Short break in a meeting, most commonly used when the meeting has lasted a long time and people need a break. It is also used when the board needs time to conduct some business, such as counting votes, during which members need not be present during. See also Take a recess.

Reconsider Motion to review a previous decision and vote on it again. It must be made by a person who voted on the prevailing (winning) side, and it requires a majority vote. Reconsideration may not be moved more than once on the same motion.

Refer to committee Instruct a committee to do research on a matter and report its findings back to the group.

	The chair may either refer the matter to an existing committee or create a new committee.
Regular meeting	Scheduled meeting of an organization.
Rescind	Nullify a vote taken at a previous meeting. A motion to rescind can be made by anyone, but only if no action has been taken on the motion. It requires a two-thirds vote for adoption.
Roll call	Calling the names of the members of an organization.
Second	Indication that a member wants a motion discussed by the membership. The member says, "I second the motion" or "Second."
Session	Meeting or group of meetings devoted to a single order of business, in which each meeting continues the work of the one before it.
Shall the question be stated?	How the question about considering a subject is discussed.
Special meeting	Meeting called to discuss a specific topic or topics. Only those items indicated in the meeting notice may be discussed.
Subsidiary motion	Motion that helps dispose of a main motion.
Table	Motion to place a main motion and all pending amendments aside temporarily, with the intention of bringing them back at a later time for action. Tabling a motion requires a second, is not debatable, cannot be amended, and requires a majority vote. Tabling a motion cannot be used to defeat a main motion by disposing of it permanently.
Take a recess	Motion providing for a short intermission in the proceedings of the organization. It needs a second, may be amended, and is passed by majority vote. See also Recess.
Take from the table	Motion to bring a previously tabled motion back before the assembly. It requires a second, is not debatable, cannot be amended, and requires a majority vote.

Tellers	Members selected to tally votes.
Time and place at which to adjourn	Motion that provides for the time and place of the next meeting. It is usually imposed only in the case of a temporary organization that does not have a regular meeting schedule. Passing this motion does not serve to adjourn the meeting.
Treasurer's report	Financial report of an organization.
Two-thirds vote	This occurs when there are twice as many people voting "Yes" as those who are voting "No." For instance, assume there are 100 people in a meeting and only 15 vote. If 10 vote "Yes" and 5 vote "No," the motion will be passed by a two-thirds vote.
Unanimous consent	This occurs when no one objects to a motion. Unanimous consent can also be called *general agreement*.
Unfinished business	Any matter pending at the time the previous meeting was adjourned. It also includes any questions that may have been postponed to the present meeting.
Withdraw a motion	Take back a motion one has made. A person may withdraw a motion by merely requesting to do so up until the time it is stated by the chair. After the chair has stated the motion, the person who made it can withdraw it only by the consent of the members.